W9-CBH-450

Brooks — Cork Library
Shelton State
Community College
DISCARDED

DATE DUE

DEMCO, INC. 38-2931

THE BOTTOM LINE ON INTEGRITY

QUINN McKAY

THE BOTTOM LINE ON
INTEGRITY

12 PRINCIPLES

FOR HIGHER

RETURNS

Brooks — Cork Library
Shelton State
Community College

DISCARDED

Gibbs Smith, Publisher
Salt Lake City

This book is dedicated to the most important associates in my life: Shirley, my wife of unquestionable devotion, and my children: Shirene McKay Bell, Cathy McKay Salisbury, David and Toni McKay, Maryann and Daniel Goodsell, Rebecca and Jay Meyer, and also eleven cherished grandchildren.

First Edition
08 07 06 05 04   5 4 3 2 1

Text © 2004 Quinn McKay

All rights reserved. No part of this book may be reproduced by
any means whatsoever without written permission from the publisher,
except brief portions quoted for purpose of review.

Published by
Gibbs Smith, Publisher
P.O. Box 667
Layton, Utah 84041

Orders: 1.800.748.5439
www.gibbs-smith.com

Printed and bound in the U.S.A.

Library of Congress Cataloging-in-Publication Data

McKay, Quinn G., 1926-
The bottom line on integrity : 12 principles for higher
returns /Quinn McKay.– 1st ed.
     p. cm.
Includes bibliographical references.
ISBN 1-58685-380-5
1. Business ethics. I. Title.
HF5387.M4315 2004
174'.4–dc22   2004008160

CONTENTS

ACKNOWLEDGMENTS

While it is my name that appears on the cover of this book, seldom does such a work, large or small, result from the efforts of a single person. In my case, the efforts of many, over a period of years, combined to produce this book.

The naming of each one is an impossibility. Nevertheless, I feel though my thanks may be brief and limited to only a representative sampling of those who contributed to this writing, I need to make my thanks a matter of public record.

I owe a great debt of gratitude to my immediate family—my wife Shirley who over the years gave invaluable suggestions. When at times my interest would flag, she supplied the encouragement to pick up the project again and move forward. My children lent praise and urgency to the cause just at the time of need, particularly David who lent his typing and considerable writing skills as well as material and ideas.

Also there is an extended family of seven brothers and sisters and their spouses who showed great forbearance and gave valuable responses in the face of my incessant discussions of ethics and values over the years: Donna and Gunn McKay, Lucy and Monroe McKay, Elaine and Barrie McKay, Ann and George Downs, Mary and Jerold Stirland, Elizabeth and Brent Seamons, Williamena and Del Richardson, as well as some fifty nieces and nephews. Most of the time, I'm sure they thought I was just playing games, but their responses and challenges helped me greatly mature ideas that would have been much less without them.

My close professional associates, particularly Bruce Bennett, president of STAR corporation, David Tippetts, Glade Tuckett, Chris Marshall, and their wives gave unusual support not just as sounding boards but through their professional encouragement, along with anecdotes, to give life to valuable ideas.

I thank the officers of the Salt Lake Rotary Club, notably John Bennion, who gave me opportunities to make formal presentations of my concepts in connection with Rotary's Four Way Test. My table partners at the club's weekly luncheons over the years endured my obsession with the project in cheerful repartee and gave me real insights into the complexity of the practical application of the principles of integrity in the workaday business world. Other professionals were particularly helpful: Arland Larsen (who still regularly sends me articles and ideas), Chaude Smith, Ivan Radman, Cyril Figuerees, Alan Tingey, and Wendell Child who explored concepts with me and motivated me with the periodic prod, "When is that book going to be finished?"

Jerry Useem, a reporter for *Fortune* magazine, through extended conversations, helped test my concepts and proved to be an unusually fine model of writing. He also generously allowed me to use a vital anecdote in the book.

Many students I have had over the years pushed back on their professor to clarify ideas that initially were vague and unfocused. Executives and managers in many organizations where I have conducted training seminars have shared their experiences and specific incidents that helped illuminate the concepts of this book. This has especially been the case with my ongoing relationship with the L3 Communications Corporation.

Kelly Cowser played a special role in the book's production, typing every page of this book and retyping many while doing editing in the process, sometimes under the pressure of deadline, with the cheerful response, "Sure we can do that." Her husband Steve and four children added to the pleasantness of the team effort as they willingly passed on pages and messages to carry the project to fulfillment.

Several authors and publishers have been more than generous in allowing materials to be used in this work, including quotes, anecdotes, cases, and studies. Excerpts from their works have added immeasurably to make this writing much more than it would have otherwise been.

People linking a chain of events going back thirty years have played critical roles in bringing this book to fruition and to them I am deeply indebted. In the early 1970s, Saul B. Sells, director of the Institute for Behavioral Research at Texas Christian University, invited me to prepare and make a three-hour presentation on "Business Ethics" to a group of twenty-nine senior business executives. The work on that project was seminal in whetting my interest and launching years of research on the subject. Trent Price, then an editor with Executive Excellence Publishing, did the yeoman's effort in producing my original book on the subject and gave me valuable training in the process. Alan Yuspeh, then executive director of the Defense Industry Initiative, took a special interest in the manuscript of that original book, and since then has continued to be a valued professional and personal friend on this matter of integrity.

More recently, for months my friend Rudell "Bud" Willey urged me to write again. Finally, it was he who boldly took me and made a personal introduction to Gibbs Smith, owner of Gibbs Smith, Publisher. Mr. Smith's immediate interest introduced me to Christopher Robbins, general manager, who proved a great coach in outlining what could be done. When the writing became a reality, I was placed in the professional and caring hands of editors Madge Baird and Johanna Buchert Smith. Indeed, they carried off the exhausting burden of maturing a manuscript for final printing with great expertise and cheerful, sensitive encouragement. Their personal association has been a rewarding experience to me. Other staff at Gibbs Smith, many of whom I have not even met, have contributed to design, title, and other matters that have created a work that is much better than I had expected. Those staff I have encountered at every level, including Debbie Uribe at the receptionist workplace, have been most congenial, making an otherwise arduous task a most pleasant one.

When it comes to the bottom line, however, the responsibility for the concepts, the interpretation of the materials I have borrowed, and the conclusions reached rest with the author. And, if no other value comes from writing this book than simply that it has been the stimulus for others to develop better ideas of their own, my effort has been worthwhile.

INTRODUCTION

PRACTICALLY EVERY DAY more corporations, institutions, and individuals of responsibility are exposed with their hands in the cookie jar of scandal and unsavory behavior.

Surveys have shown that "three quarters to 98 percent of college students [have] admitted to cheating in high school.... According to an exclusive *U.S. News* poll, 84 percent of college students believe they need to cheat to get ahead in the world today."[1] In our citadels of honor, the military academies, scandalous behavior has been made public. Studies of medical doctors have revealed that when faced with specific situations, a significant percent would lie to payment agencies for their patient's benefit. Glancing through the business section of a recent newspaper, I counted no less than five articles on the first two pages with headlines about fraud and the indictment of corporate officers, and reports of a major company being punished by the government for stealing sensitive information from a competitor.

As unsettling as the numbers are, the more disturbing aspect is which institutions are exhibiting this lack of integrity. Sadly, among the list of those caught in scandalous behavior are many of our most preeminent institutions. Arthur Andersen, until recently, was regarded as the number one professional auditing firm, not only for its professional expertise, but also for its exemplary integrity. Since its inside workings were brought to light, not only has the organization's reputation been destroyed but also its very existence. Curiosity begs the question, how many auditing firms have been basically doing what Andersen did, but are still functioning? And it hasn't been just Andersen. Contemplate some of the other illustrious names whose integrity has been called into public question: Coca Cola, Merrill Lynch, Boeing Airplane, Royal Dutch Shell, the *New York Times,* several universities, and even the institutions we rely on to be the trusted caretakers of all that is moral—churches. Even here, the preeminent institution—the Roman Catholic Church—fell prey, over an extended period of time, to serious moral indiscretions.

There is evidence all around that these failures of integrity can and do occur among the reputable as well as the disreputable, with large, long-established institutions as well as small fly-by-nighters, and the high and the mighty as well as the lowly with little standing in our society.

The results-oriented philosophy that impels our society may in part explain our predicament. Some three hundred years ago, Baltasar Gracian, a Spanish Jesuit, wrote, "Win affection . . . learn how to be evasive. . . . To enslave our natural superiors by use of cunning is a novel kind of power, among the best that life can offer."

He continues, "A victor needs no explanations. The majority do not look closely into circumstantial detail, but only at a successful or unsuccessful outcome; thus, one's reputation never suffers if one's object is obtained."[2]

Two examples may help demonstrate how this is still true in our twenty-first century business culture.

■ DON'T ASK, DON'T TELL

A man I will call Abner Sebald decided to leave his partnership in the retail office supplies world. He looked around for the best opportunity he could find to make it on his own, and he finally decided to acquire an auto dealership that was available for purchase in town. He knew little of the automobile business, but he was an excellent salesman and was well known and well liked in the community. One person said about him, "Anyone can trust Abner." So, Abner acquired the business, and over the next several years he became successful far beyond his dreams.

After almost twenty years of success in the automobile business, and after his having become a man of influence in his home state, I called on him and found him to be in a rare solemn mood. As we sat on a bench in front of his business, he related to me an experience that was obviously troubling him.

When he had first purchased the dealership, recognizing his ignorance of the business, he had asked a few experienced auto dealers in the area, "What are the keys to success in this business?" He soon got the message that dealerships are made or broken on the used car lot. Reselling the trade-ins was the key. He resolved to find a top manager for the used cars. He kept hearing about one Joe Steritt who had been managing a used car lot in a neighboring state. He became acquainted with the man and made him a very attractive offer. Joe lived up to his reputation; in a short time the business became highly profitable.

To increase car sales, the company would occasionally send two or three employees to California to buy good used cars, drive them back, and refurbish them before selling them. The "ringer" cars often brought in customers just to see what was available, and sometimes those customers would make a purchase. The dealership's reputation was improving.

Just a few days before our conversation, Abner explained, Joe, another employee, and Abner's son Brad (home for the summer from graduate school) had just returned from such a trip. Just after they had arrived back at the shop, Brad approached his father and asked, "Dad, I want to know if you really believe all those things you taught me about honesty or if it was just talk?"

"What do you mean?" asked Abner, somewhat startled.

"Well, while we were driving back here, Joe told me how he markets these cars. He said he turns the odometers back on some of them. [This incident took place before federal laws prohibited this practice.] He says that on the Ford with 80,000 miles, he is going to make it 45,000."

After the conversation, Abner called Joe over to him and said feebly, "Now Joe, we have talked before about turning back the odometers . . ."

"Yeah, I know," Joe interrupted. "But you want this part of the business to be profitable, right? And that car is a lot better car than the 80,000 miles on the dash show."

Abner told me that it had immediately become evident to his son that although his father advocated high standards of honesty, he had tolerated something lower on the used-car side of the business. When it came down to it, Abner only checked the profitability of the lot and avoided making any inquiries about the day-to-day practices of "someone who knows how to manage a used-car lot successfully." This discrepancy, finally pointed out to him after more than twenty years, was what caused Abner's somber mood that day. To this day, Abner is regarded as one of the two or three most honest businesspeople in the city. But it seemed to me that, at least for a while after this incident, he didn't feel that way.

A former legislative staffer—I'll call him Derek—shared his experience with me over lunch.

During his six years in Washington, D.C., Derek served on the staff of a prominent senator and then on the staff of a congressman. While working for the senator, Derek explained that one of his primary responsibilities was to open mail. He told how the senator received about 2,000 letters a month from his constituents and additional mail from people who were not of his constituency but who wanted his attention for some cause or concern. The senator never saw most of the letters. Instead, the staff would open the mail and read it and then write a reply as though the senator himself was responding. Derek would use "the senator's personal signature stamp, stamp the letter in the appropriate place, and send it off." Neither the original letter nor the reply were ever seen by the senator.

"Sometimes," Derek continued, "someone who had received one of the letters would come to Washington and make an appointment to see the senator. When this happened, we would scurry around, find the letter and the reply, place them on the senator's desk, and then brief the senator on the issues just before the constituent came into his office." Once the constituent was in the senator's office, he or she usually thanked him for his prompt reply to the letter. By now, the senator was familiar with the correspondence, and so he never mentioned that he hadn't seen the correspondence until that day. The constituent would leave feeling very good about all the "personal" attention received. This reputation for giving personal attention to each person's correspondence was very valuable for the senator. "I actually have been in the offices and homes of some of the senator's constituents," said Derek, "who have the senator's 'personal' letters tacked to the wall or framed. They point to the signature with pride and tell me how they received a 'personal' letter from the senator."

One of the justifications Derek gave for this artifice was that "everybody does it that way." Well, not quite. Maybe it would be more accurate to say that most people or perhaps only many in Washington answer mail that way. After all, Derek also told me about his experience in the congressman's office.

Derek explained that the congressman's office handled mail in much the same way as the senator's office had. However, one day a constituent came to the office, and the staff put the pertinent letter and reply on the congressman's desk. Later, when the constituent referred to the congressman's letter, the congressman immediately interrupted and said, "You need to know that I did not write this letter. These letters are all written by my staff. I seldom even see them. That's just the way the system works around here."

Are these congressional delegates honest? Does a person of integrity in public office deliberately lead constituents to believe that they have enjoyed the personal attention of a senator when no such thing happened? In some circles, claiming authorship for something written by another is called forgery or plagiarism.

This particular senator publicly rails against people who deliberately mislead, deceive, obfuscate, or lie. He preaches the importance of honesty and integrity. The congressman seems less willing to perpetrate the ruse when face-to-face with his constituents, but he still allows communications to go out over his signature when he is unaware of either the letter or the reply—a pretense that conveys a false impression.

If these elected officials want to be truthful, why don't they just be forthcoming about this policy and have their staff be honest and up front? In their letter writing, they could explain to the constituents how impossible it is for a senator or congressman to respond personally to such a large volume of mail, and so the responsibility to reply to the letter has been given to staff members. The staff member could then respond to the letter and sign it with his or her own signature and title, "Chief letter answerer for the senator."

If such forthrightness does not seem appropriate, then maybe we can acknowledge that the practice of letter writing for someone else is deceptive, even dishonest, but it maintains a necessary image and reputation of giving personal attention to people that is critical for a politician's effectiveness. In other words, the effectiveness of a powerful person is more important than honesty in this case. In any case, we can at least be honest with ourselves.

■ THIS BOOK

In this writing, I will attempt to give some insight into how reputable organizations can go bad. Also, how some institutions maintain good reputations while engaging in dubious moral practices.

When speaking of integrity, I will give emphasis to its three major ingredients: 1) honesty, 2) trustworthiness, and 3) consistency or predictability. Most dictionaries include honesty as the first element of integrity. Then they refer to being whole or integrated in structure. For us, this means being consistent in what we say and what we do—"walking the talk." If individuals act with integrity, expressing their values in their behavior, others have a good basis for predicting how they will behave in a given circumstance.

Twelve keys to creating a house or institution of integrity are identified in this book. Each chapter describes the concept of one of them and explores its ramifications. They are the following:

Key #1:   Rise above trite slogans that feed self-deception.

Key #2:   Agree on a working definition of truth telling.

Key #3:   Be wary of four devices of deception.

Key #4:   Recognize pressure as a major determinant
of honesty.

Key #5:   Be alert to incremental morality.

Key #6:   Realize that everyone lives by two different
ethical standards.

Key #7:   Develop the essential skills for personal integrity.

Key #8:   Resolve conflicts of principle: there are no gray areas.

Key #9:   Create a climate where wrongful acts can be reported.

Key #10:   Understand the law of obligation.

Key #11:   Know when a promise is a promise.

Key #12:   Allow that lying is sometimes the right thing to do.

A PRACTICAL APPROACH

While many books on integrity and ethics emphasize the teachings of philosophers, this book forgoes that approach. Philosophers have good things to say, but learning to apply moral values to our daily business dealings is the greater challenge and needs the greater help. It is so easy for most of us to agree and feel comfortable discussing matters in general philosophical terms. But being able to apply the generalization to a specific situation—where the rubber meets the road—that's where the difficulty arises and where the help is needed.

For this reason, in the chapters and at the end of each chapter are specific incidents to be used for staff or employee discussions. By getting beyond the abstract to the practical, employers will have a meaningful opportunity to help those they lead understand the priority of values in their institutions. This is very important because values often conflict with each other and members of a group need to know how they are expected to handle such conflicts. Also, discussing practical situations helps to alert members of confusing circumstances that will arise. Being able to anticipate conflicts helps people not be caught off guard by surprises.

All of the incidents and cases cited are actual situations, although I have disguised the names and locations in some of them; these writings are not intended to be an exposé of any specific person or institution's wrongdoing. Rather, I cite actual incidents to gain insights, clarify by example, demonstrate concepts, and develop guidelines for appropriate behavior.

Although most find it comfortable to point the finger at "those wrongdoers" (e.g., Bill Clinton, Enron officers, Martha Stewart, or whomever), improving integrity in our society really begins with me. Too many people point to government leaders, other business executives, public figures, and the guy across the street as the dishonest bad boys. At the same time, they see themselves as basically honest, not in need of change like that man down the road. Recognizing that you have room for improvement is an essential first step.

The writer/preacher John Donne put it well when he said, "How many men that stand at an execution, if they would ask, 'For what dies this man?' should hear their own faults condemned, and see themselves executed by attorney? . . . I may lack much of the good parts of the meanest, but I lack nothing of the morality of the weakest; they may have acquired better abilities than I, but I was born to as many infirmities as they."[3]

I have often found that just helping people become aware that their behavior lacks integrity, without preaching explicitly, results in their taking steps to act with greater integrity on their own. At a recent seminar I gave, I attempted to set appropriate expectations by saying, "I do not expect you to leave this class and be totally honest. As a result of attending this class, if this next week you will act more honestly in just one matter than you would have done otherwise, I will feel we have been successful."

The next day a dentist who was attending handed me a small plastic bag. Inside was a California disabled person parking placard, (cut in half), with a note: "Success is yours! I am one person who took one principle home and made one honest change in my life." He explained to me how, though not disabled, he had obtained the placard to help solve the difficulty of trying to find a parking stall. The pressure of his work schedule had apparently pushed him to this creative solution.

Helping people become aware of their own behavior and recognize the implications of honesty and integrity can result in moral improvement. Self-awareness of behavior and recognition of the personal implications of honesty and integrity is a primary objective of this book. If you and your employees can be persuaded—or provoked—to do some self-analysis, to think about your behavior in ways you have never thought before, then self-improvement and an improved morality in your company will occur.

■ HOW TO USE THIS BOOK

When it comes to integrity, the big challenge is how to ingrain the desired values into team members' behavior. Using this book can help ingrain integrity by: 1) individual study or 2) group training. The most effective would be 3) a combination of 1 and 2.

1) Requiring team members to read the book individually will introduce concepts and vocabulary that will encourage a better understanding of the many facets of integrity and enable meaningful discussion. Individual reading will motivate insights into one's own behavior and begin a necessary self-evaluation.

2) Using the book for integrity education in formal training programs or staff meetings will create enlightened thinking and reinforce desired behavior. One session won't do the job. A series of sessions (one for each "key") will be necessary for any significant effect.

Assign ahead of time incidents found at the end of each chapter or those embedded within the chapter text. Ask team members to come to the training session prepared to say what they would do if they were faced with this situation and explain why. These incidents can be used with good effect—on the spot—without a previous assignment when desired. Just read the incident out loud with others following their own copy. This is a good approach when "integrity" is just one of several items on a staff meeting agenda.

Let as many team members express their proposed action and analysis as possible. Let participants challenge each other's ideas by pointing out unrecognized implications their actions may cause. The team leader should be prepared to raise questions overlooked by team members. There are suggested questions following each "case." This open exchange provokes a self-awareness and lasting impact that lecturing often fails to do.

In the course of discussion, people often introduce their own experience in their institutions. This is good. It will enhance the lessons with the here-and-now application. It also provides an opportunity for executives and managers to insert and defend their expectations on such aspects as a definition of honesty, handling conflicts, or coping with pressures, etc.

For best results, I strongly urge that you start this discussion training with the top executives first and then work down the organization: a) This will give key executives the opportunity to convey their refined values and expectations to the team leaders who will carry the training throughout the organization. An outside consultant or professional can often be helpful in this introductory step to "train the trainers," b) this approach will send an important message that this matter is very important to this institution, c) this will help clarify and increase understanding of an organization's rules and policies, and d) this approach will also provide consistent instruction at each level and will encourage administrative action that reinforces the values that have been taught. In other words, it will encourage a walking of the talking. The alternative, pushing values from the bottom up, is like overcoming gravity—very difficult.

3) The combination of individual study and group discussion will be most effective in producing desired results. If only one is possible, group discussion will have a much greater impact than individual study alone.

The concepts detailed in this book are intended to help individuals and groups wrestle more constructively and effectively with the challenges to integrity in their day-to-day business lives. I hope you will find the wrestle as stimulating and challenging as I have.

Enjoy the wrestle—and the positive results!

RISE ABOVE TRITE
SLOGANS THAT FEED
SELF-DECEPTION

CHAPTER ONE

Integrity Begins with Being Honest About Dishonesty

WHILE I WAS WRITING a chapter for this book, Ken Cross came to my house to repair an appliance. Ken told me he owned his own appliance repair business and was a franchisee of the Sears Repair Service. "The Sears name gives my small business an immediate good image," he said.

Shortly, he noticed the papers spread about the desk and on the floor and asked what I was doing. When he learned I was writing a book about integrity, he quickly volunteered, "That's one thing I feel very strongly about in running my business—*always be honest.*"

Wanting to know what he meant by his statement and how it applied in his business, I asked, "Do you think lying is sometimes the right thing for an honest person to do?"

His response was, "Definitely not. Never!"

Then I described three real-life situations where acting in strict honesty would cause serious damage to people or even loss of life.

After a thoughtful pause, and in a somewhat subdued voice, he said, "Oh dear, I've never thought about honesty in that way."

In the classes I teach, seminars, lectures, and in private conversations, this is the most frequent response I hear: "I've just never *thought* about that." Why have people never thought seriously in a below-the-surface way about integrity and honesty? One major reason is that people are so given to indulging in trite slogans. Each of us needs to hear more than recited slogans to establish a culture of integrity. Yet how often do we hear leaders dismiss a challenge to honesty with a statement such as:

- Honesty is always the best policy.
- The only way to get ahead in business is to be honest.
- If you lie, you will get caught.
- Just be honest.
- Respect others.
- Just live the Golden Rule.
- Be loyal.

◼ WHEN YOU RELY ON SLOGANS

Many years ago, one of my professors made a statement I have found to be quite insightful: "Slogans and platitudes are thought stoppers." That is, when you can phrase a slogan or platitude that people will pick up and repeat, people will stop thinking about or analyzing the actual subject. This failure to give serious analytical thought to the matter of integrity is a major barrier to those who would develop within themselves and their businesses a culture of integrity.

If you went to your doctor feeling poorly, and the doctor said only, after some observations, "Yes, you are sick. Now go home and be healthy. Good health pays," surely you would be disappointed if not upset. Such pithy advice bears little fruit. You would rightly expect your doctor to identify what is wrong, what is the cause, and then coach you on what to do to get better and to stay well.

Sometimes it seems that business execs sling slogans with little thought. Slogans are even built into company policy and culture with printed documents and oral recitations. One national healthcare organization published in its mission and values statement: "We act with absolute honesty, integrity, and fairness in the way we conduct our business and the way we live our lives." Another major insurance company declares in one of its brochures, "Our *people* are steeped in a century-and-a-half of *integrity*. Our long history has proven *sound ethics* is good business."

John Abbott Worthley, a writer and consultant on ethics, calls such talk "ethics prattle." "When it comes to ethics, it is relatively simple to talk a good line, generously spouting splendid sounding terms like 'principles,' 'integrity,' and 'the highest standards.' "[1]

But glossing over the real challenges of integrity with vague generalities does not create a corporation of integrity. Those who aspire for an institution of integrity must rise above preachy slogans and learn the anatomy of integrity.

■ LABELS DON'T TELL THE WHOLE STORY

It would seem a truism to say that all people are honest at times and all people are dishonest at times. But if this is so, what is meant by the statement, "She is an honest person," or "He is a dishonest person?"

Labels, like slogans, are often a distraction that keep people from serious thought about integrity.

In a university class on business ethics, I asked my students to define what it means to be an honest person. A feeble mental struggle ensued. Do you have to be 100 percent honest to merit the title? Honest 95 percent of the time? Will 75 percent or 51 percent do? What about the week when I was totally honest, except for just one lie? What if that one lie was just a little white one? What if the single lie was a whopper? What if it was just middle-sized? We agreed not to use the term *honest person* until the class had devised a useful definition. Three months later when the class concluded, no student was willing to use the term.

We live in a peculiar society, ethically. Without being cynical, ponder the idea that just possibly it would be more helpful to encourage our employees to cultivate a "reputation" for honesty rather than stress always *actually* being honest. You might retort, "Well, they are the same thing; being honest in all things is how one gets a reputation of honesty." That seems like an idea worth testing.

When a group is asked to cite a historical incident that epitomizes honesty, to what do most refer? Most frequently it is the story of the boy George Washington cutting down the cherry tree. Apparently, however, historical researchers have concluded that the event never occurred. It is a fascinating irony that we teach the importance of honesty by reciting a falsehood. Little wonder that with preachy slogans regularly triggering our senses, youth and adults alike find insecurity and confusion when they strive for a life of integrity.

Statements, announcements, memos and even printed manuals on their own will not do the job. Serious truth tellers know it requires serious, meaningful, on-going discussions—backed up by the appropriate administrative practices—to instill integrity in an organization. It takes the application of major resources over an extended period of time to create an institution of integrity. Then more attention and resources are essential to maintain that house of integrity.

An occasional memo does not cause a company to become cost-conscious or profit-focused. It takes the same effort to create a business of integrity as it does to make a business consistently profitable. Without meaningful talk, goals, commitment, creativity, regular measurement, and checkups, it will not happen. Regular training and a regular spot on the agenda for staff meetings are essential for two reasons:

1) To clarify what this organization really means by integrity and to make sure it is understood.
2) To establish through consistent attention that integrity is valued and a priority. Irregular and infrequent attention signals that it is a low priority.

Not long ago, the vice president of a national company invited me to help with ethical training for the company's employees. After my planning visit with the vice president, he gave me a very attractive manual that laid out in detail the policies, guidelines, and rules for ethical behavior in this company. A day later, after having studied the manual, I was so impressed with the contents that it prompted me to phone the vice president. "Wendel, why do you need me?" I asked. "You already have an excellent, comprehensive manual on ethics." He said, "Quinn, I know that, but it just sits on the shelves. Our staff meetings are consumed with concerns about costs and how to improve profits. We never take time to discuss concerns about ethics and integrity unless some legal trouble arises. It seems that we are telling our employees that integrity is just not that important. Costs are what's important."

A pronouncement, memo, or well-worded slogan, or even a well-printed manual does no more to establish integrity in a company than laying one brick does to create a mansion.

Strangely, in all my years of consulting, teaching, and working in business, I have never met a dishonest manager. Everyone I have asked has attested to his or her personal integrity. So where are the dishonest people?

Overcoming self-deception and becoming aware of the anatomy of integrity is an essential first step to creating a house of integrity. If honesty in our society is going to improve, it's not going to start with Arthur Andersen, Enron, Bill Clinton, Carl Ponzi, or Saddam Hussein—or my competitor down the street. Only when I recognize that it starts with me will progress be made. People continue to cite others' dishonesty and seldom focus on the times they themselves have been untruthful.

An example of how far this self-deception can go and how complete it can become is demonstrated by a conversation I had some time ago with a retired executive. He had spent many years with one of the best-known retail chains in the United States and insisted, "In my forty-three years with my company, I have never engaged in one unethical act—nor has my company."

When I asked, "Do you really mean that neither you nor your organization has ever done one unethical thing?" he responded, "Not even once."

The conversation continued for another twenty to thirty minutes, during which time I presented several business situations with multiple ethical dimensions, and I asked him what he would do. He was able to recall in detail some of the past practices of his company, and we discussed some relevant ethical principles. Near the end of our discussion, he volunteered, "Well, I had never thought about our activities in that way before. I guess I will have to go back and do some rethinking about ethics."

This man was no scheming or conniving "dishonest" manager. He had only been the apparent victim of the "what we are doing is ethical" trap. We are seduced into believing that our actions are ethical because someone in power over us says that it's fine. It seems that in many cases people reason, "I am an honest person; therefore, what I do must be honest and ethical."

The incident that really started my personal quest to understand integrity can be traced to several years ago, when I presented a half-day program on business ethics to an executive development program at Texas Christian University. At the start of my program I asked a few questions, sort of a pre-test so I could find out generally where the group stood on the subject. The first question I asked the twenty-nine top executives was, "How many of you consider yourself an honest

In another incident during a discussion about bribery in a business ethics class, a woman who held a supervisory position in a government office told the other class members how the rules in her office were so strict that no one was allowed to accept any gifts. "We can't even accept so much as a calendar," she said and continued by sharing her strong personal endorsement of the rule, emphasizing her own high standards of ethics and how important it is to obey the rules.

Later in the same class, the discussion turned to the ethical problems in obeying or not obeying the law. Most of the students felt that disobeying the law was generally to be considered unethical behavior. At this point, the woman who would not accept a calendar as a gift told the class that she and her husband regularly and knowingly hired illegal aliens to help out in their small home-based business. She justified herself by saying, "It's ethical to give these people an opportunity to make a living."

person?" All twenty-nine hands went up. Then I asked, "How many of you engage in dishonest business practices?" Not one raised a hand. And finally, "How many of you have encountered dishonest people in the course of your work?" All twenty-nine hands were raised again.

For about three hours, the group wrestled with actual business situations. The executives were asked to judge whether some common business practices were "honest" or "dishonest." They were able to identify cases of deception: the deliberate misleading of customers, competitors, and creditors; the withholding of information to avoid a true impression; consciously delaying payment to creditors beyond the agreed-upon due date; and so forth.

At the conclusion of the session, I again asked the participants, "How many of you consider yourself an honest person?" Three hands went up, and then I followed, "How many of you engage in dishonest practices?" Twenty-six hands went up. It was interesting to see the change from their initial judgment where, without hesitation, the whole group had been able to spot the dishonest tendencies and behaviors of the people we discussed, but they had not yet found those same tendencies toward dishonesty in their own behavior. When I asked how they had been able to reconcile such apparent incongruities, many responded with, "I just hadn't looked at it that way before," or "I just wasn't aware that it was dishonest before."

If you desire to be a force for raising the level of integrity in your company, you must at least be honest with yourself, acknowledging privately if not publicly, that you have indulged in dishonesty. *Integrity begins with being honest about dishonesty.*

Brooks – Cork Library
Shelton State
Community College

There is a principle of human behavior that helps explain our tendency toward self-deception. Because the concept will also be referred to in later chapters, I will introduce it here.

"Most people find it significantly easier to recall pleasant and satisfying experiences than mildly disturbing or mildly unpleasant experiences. This psychological characteristic, which enables man to ignore or block out certain experiences while recognizing and retaining a consciousness of others is called **selective perception**."[2]

When evidence or questions arise that would suggest we are not being objective, fair, or honest, we tend to blank out the evidence or refuse to answer the question. This relieves us of the mental anguish that would come from recognizing the problem.

For instance, someone may make a less-than-honest statement in order to be true to an obligation. Since most people see themselves as trustworthy in their obligations and friendships *and* honest in their speech, when these principles come into conflict with each other (as they often do), the mind seeks to eliminate the internal conflict by "blanking out" the idea that perhaps they have made a false statement.

According to ethics writer David Cherrington, if I sincerely believe that I am basically honest all the time, but my words or behavior begin to conflict with this belief, psychologically it will be much easier for me to redefine honesty—and by so doing keep my record of honesty perfect—than to admit to dishonesty and then try to correct all my errors by confronting family, peers, bosses, customers, suppliers, the public, and so forth.

> Selective perception in a capsule:
> 1) People see and often enhance that which is satisfying.
> 2) People tend to ignore and blank out that which is mildly disturbing.
> 3) People again see mildly disturbing things when they become persistent or dangerous.

This tendency to rationalize and justify rather than correct and modify leads to an interesting phenomenon: Many people in prisons, who have been caught red-handed in acts of fraud or embezzlement still claim from the depths of their jail cells, in all sincerity, "I am basically an honest person," or "I got a bad rap."

Similarly, senior executives perched high atop their luxury office suites built on the backs of their defrauded and often powerless past business associates still insist, "This company values the highest standards of integrity and good character." Such is the power of selective perception.[3]

The selective perception phenomenon explains how the CEO of a major corporation, Geoffrey C. Bible, can sincerely state in *Business Week:*

> "There is going to be a Day of Judgment. If there isn't a day up there, it's when you're lying on your deathbed. And you're going to say to yourself: 'Well, what did I achieve in my life?' It's not how much you've made, or how big a house you've got, or how many cars. It's what you did for your fellow man. It's 'What did I do to make the world better?' That's what it's going to come down to."[4]

Because of selective perception, Bible can, with all sincerity, proclaim these lofty words and thoughts all the while his company is producing, promoting, and selling to the public a product that causes the premature death of hundreds of thousands of people every year. Mr. Bible is the CEO of the Phillip Morris Tobacco Company, which in addition to tobacco interests, also has programs that help people improve their lives and health.

A person's or company's reputation is often built on selective perception. For instance, Abraham Lincoln has the reputation in our society as "Honest Abe." Having a clear recall of this oft-repeated label, most people in our society can cite one or more incidents of his honest behavior. However, scarcely a one can cite an incident of his dishonesty. Is this because he never did one dishonest thing? Hardly. Serious historians do mention his tendency to obfuscate and stretch the truth. However, selective perception causes us to brightly remember the former and to blank out the latter and thus allow us to sincerely maintain the "Honest Abe" image. In fact, it would seem that anyone who has the audacity to point out an incidence of Lincoln's dishonesty is surely a liar and unpatriotic.

This phenomenon also operates to the detriment of one with a negative reputation. For instance, for many, former President Bill Clinton was and is a liar. They can point to specific incidents of dishonesty because of what they have read and heard about him. When these people are asked to cite examples of his honesty, they often draw a blank. When most people have arrived at a conclusion of honesty or dishonesty, they recall only those instances that reinforce their judgment. The tendency to blank out other insightful data allows them to take that position sincerely.

We do the same thing for ourselves and our businesses when we notice only the times we are honest, and actually ignore or push out of our consciousness any recollection of our dishonest acts.

■ STARTING TOWARD INTEGRITY HONESTLY

Most people (and by extension their companies) start out with the premise, "I am not a liar. I am an honest person." Then, rather than acknowledge to themselves actions of deceit, lying, or dishonesty, they exercise their minds—often very creatively—to justify their self-image of being an honest person. This leads to a search for slogans, labels, and words—nuanced, subtle, and self-deceptive—to articulate their original self-image. With these newfound words, we not only reinforce their self-deception, but we also verbally arm ourselves to "honestly" justify our self-deception to others rather than pursue a serious self-evaluation. This process allows a Richard Nixon to declare to the world in all sincerity, "I am not a crook."

It allowed a friend of mine to engage in a similar self-deception. She and her husband operate a successful small business related to the construction industry. In a recent discussion on integrity, she earnestly, sincerely, and with vigor stated, "Yes, I do lie sometimes, but I am not a liar!"

To be a serious truth teller and make serious efforts to create an institution of integrity, one must rise above such statements that feed self-deception and distract one from the serious concerns of integrity.

CASE: THE $400 SUIT[5]

With experience, salespeople can become accurate judges of their prospective customers. So when Sam Morris saw a breezy character striding into City Clothing Store, where he was employed, he identified the customer as someone who would say just what he wanted to buy, and make up his mind quickly. He guessed right. The customer promptly informed Sam what type and color of suit he wanted and added that he had exactly $400 to spend on a suit and would not go a cent higher.

Sam loved this kind of customer best. He could show him what was in stock and get a decision in a hurry—usually a sale—without having to drag everything off the racks and out of the back room.

At the moment though, Sam was troubled. The store's inventory was temporarily low, and Sam didn't have anything approaching what his customer wanted between $350 and $450. He knew he couldn't sell the man the $450 suit, and he was afraid that this type of customer might refuse to be convinced of the economic advantage of a $350 suit. He didn't want to lose the sale since he knew the customer had come in to buy.

So Sam told the customer to look around for a moment and went to the back of the store where he removed the price tag from the $350 suit and substituted a $400 tag. The customer liked the suit and the price, and after some custom tailoring, walked out of the store perfectly satisfied with his new suit.

QUESTIONS

1. Was Sam honest or dishonest in his behavior? Was he justified in changing the price? Is there anything wrong with charging what the market will bear (or with sending away a satisfied customer)?

2. What does $350 or $450 on a price tag mean? Does that number indicate the "value" of the item?

3. If you were Sam's department manager and you found out about this deal, would you promote him? Commend him? Say nothing? Reprimand him? Fire him?

4. If Sam were your best salesman, would your response be the same?

5. As Sam's department manager, suppose you hear that Sam has been discussing his prowess in making sales with other employees in the break room. Do you say anything to the other employees? What do your words and actions (or silence and inaction) say about your company's standards of honesty?

AGREE ON A WORKING
DEFINITION OF
TRUTH TELLING

CHAPTER TWO

Establishing a Definition
of Integrity

ONE COMMONLY HELD BELIEF that seriously distracts those who desire to create
a company of integrity is that "everyone knows when they are being dishonest." If
you believe such a statement and act on that belief, you are working under a serious handicap.

Let's look at three actual business incidents to clarify the challenge.

■   **1. THE AMERICAN ENTREPRENEUR**   "Had Kathy Taggares told the
truth, the whole truth, and nothing but the truth, she probably wouldn't have
a $32-million business today. Twelve years ago, Taggares was itching to ditch
her employer, frozen-food maker Chef Ready Foods, to start her own business. So she covertly approached Marriott International about buying one of
its salad dressing factories.

"To her utter surprise, her overtures got a warm reception. 'As a young,
single woman, I had so many doors slammed in my face,' she remembers,
'and here's Marriott, and they're taking me seriously.' Marriott was even offering to help her finance the $5-million purchase over several years. It
seemed almost too good to be true. And wouldn't you know it, it was. The
Marriott people, it slowly dawned on Taggares, erroneously believed she was
representing her employer, Chef Ready—not herself—as a sole entrepreneur. That's why they were taking her so seriously.

"To own up to the truth would almost certainly have meant another door slammed in her face. So what did Taggares do? 'They never directly asked me,' she says, 'so I let them believe what they wanted to believe'—namely, that she was negotiating on behalf of Chef Ready. 'They finally found out,' she recounts, 'and they were quite angry at the very end.' But by then, the deal had all but gone through. Another acquisition followed, and Taggares's company, KT Kitchens in Carson, California, now employs 350 people."[1]

Was Kathy honest in her dealings with Marriott? Did she make a dishonest statement? If she spoke no lie, then she must have been honest—right?

2. TRUST IS A MUST In 1984 Granite Savings & Loan was insured by the state's financial insurance agency. But the agency was scheduled to go out of business in January of the following year. In the meantime, the trust company was earnestly trying to qualify for FDIC insurance, but so far had not been able to do so. In December, one month before the dissolution of the state insurance agency, a judicial court hearing considered the situation. The bank owners argued that if they had just three more months, they could qualify for FDIC insurance and thereby preserve the depositors' savings and stay in business. Granite was well managed and profitable, and the depositors' savings were safe and secure.

However, one dangerous aspect of the case still loomed over the whole matter: If it were publicly announced that the bank's deposits were uninsured, most felt that the depositors would make a run on the bank to withdraw their funds, causing the savings and loan to close even though it was otherwise fiscally sound. That day, everyone in the courtroom—examiners, bank regulators, trust owners, lawyers, the judge, and local media representatives—agreed that in this case the ends were noble enough to justify the devious means of keeping depositors in the dark for a short time until other measures could be implemented. Their reasoning was that banks and trust companies operate on trust, and by maintaining that trust for a few months until the FDIC insurance came through, no one would be hurt and everyone would come out ahead.

So it was agreed. The media agreed that as long as no one else let the cat out of the bag, they would keep quiet—but if anyone leaked any information, they would feel free to grab the scoop and report the whole story.

Through January and February, Granite managers worked diligently to gain the important right to claim "insured by the FDIC." They applied and received word back that their application had been approved, but they would not be insured until three other conditions were met. By March, two of the three conditions had been fulfilled. The third one, "increase financial capital," had not yet occurred. But everyone was working on the problem, and they anticipated gaining the needed capital within a couple of weeks.

So confident were the managers in their ability to achieve this final requirement that in March they erected a temporary sign on the front lawn of the bank's main office. Clearly visible to everyone who traveled along the busy thoroughfare nearby were the words "This bank is FDIC approved." Technically, the statement was true.

The FDIC insurance final approval process dragged on through February, March, and into April. At that time, the judge called another hearing to evaluate the circumstances. Due to the state's open meeting law, a reporter from the community's leading television station was in attendance, and he felt it was about time that the withheld knowledge should become public knowledge. He wondered whether he should be a responsible citizen and inform the public of what he knew or run the risk of letting some other reporter get the scoop. He also felt that he would be derelict in his duty if he failed to report something as important to the community as the financial welfare of hundreds of depositors. Indeed, he reasoned, he had been wrong not to report the case last December.

The reporter decided to report the uninsured status of the trust company. When the bankers tried to persuade him otherwise, he refused their pleadings but agreed that he would not air the segment until after the close of business on Friday. The report was seen by the public on the evening news. Bank owners, state regulators, federal officials, and executives from other banks worked frantically over the weekend to avert a crisis. The fact was that if one trust company failed, it could trigger an industry-wide chain reaction of bank depositors withdrawing their funds in reaction to one perceived savings and loans violation.

Before the bank opened on Monday, arrangements had been made for the second-largest savings and loan in the state to take over the trust company's assets and become the new owners of Granite Savings & Loan, effective immediately. The new owners were FDIC insured. The local presses and television stations were thorough in informing the public of the deal, so when the bank opened on Monday morning, the smooth transition helped to avert a major crisis.

In the December meeting, did all the parties to the case act with integrity? Were they honest? What should they have done?

Were the bank managers honest when they put up the sign, "FDIC approved"? They did have a letter stating that fact.

In April, did the reporter act with integrity when he released the news that the bank was not actually insured? Was the reporter an honest person? A person of integrity?

3. IT'S FREE — EXCEPT FOR THE COST During the summer of 2003, between his junior and senior years of his university studies, Roy gained a sales position with a successful company that sold home security systems. He came to feel the quality of the product was the best being sold in the Oakland, California area where he was working. Especially, he felt this confidence considering the monthly charge the company was asking.

After hiring on, some forty of the summer hires were given very good sales training on successful door approach, explanation about the needs and benefits of this specific product, and very importantly, information on how to close a sale. From the outset, Roy said he felt uncomfortable with the sales approach. He said, "They weren't teaching us to lie outright, but some of their tactics and strategies seemed a bit dishonest to me."

The sales trainer explained, "When you talk to the person at the door, and they ask how much it costs, just tell them, 'It doesn't cost anything as long as you put our sign out.' And that's really true, since we give the equipment to them for free. You don't want to show them all the cards in your deck in the beginning. Tell them about the monthly fee later."

Roy described his experience further: "It seemed as though the successful people would be skillful at not telling people everything right at first. You had to 'build up the benefits of the system' first, so that when you finally told them the cost, they would feel as if they were getting a great deal. By telling the people over and over that the system is complimentary, they began to get excited about the system and feel ownership of it. So, when you brought up the 'small monthly cost' at 'only a dollar a day' (actually $39.99—which is really $40) for the monitoring service, they would more easily accept buying. I didn't feel that was right."

Roy tried the company's approach for a while, but he became so uncomfortable with what he regarded as "shady tactics," that he decided to be upfront with potential customers about costs and all. Others were selling two or three times as many systems as Roy. Which left him very frustrated.

Finally Roy asked for his manager's help, inviting him to accompany him to the doors. During the experience, Roy expressed to his manager that the successful approach "seemed like deception."

At this point the manager became somewhat exasperated, saying, "We're not lying to people! We tell them about the price before they sign up. It's not like we are hiding the charges from them; we just don't tell them right at the beginning. There's nothing wrong with that."

Is this company using an honest sales technique, or as Roy felt, is it shady and misleading? Is the equipment "complimentary" or is it just included in the monthly service fee? Is Roy overly sensitive about honesty or does he just not understand the difference between honesty and lying? How easy is it to identify when a person is being honest and when he or she is being deceptive?

■   SPOTTING THE LIE

Oft times, identifying a statement or action as "the truth" or "a lie" can be a fuzzy, uncertain matter. In some cases, lies are as plain as the nose on Pinocchio's face. In many more cases, they are so subtle as to be difficult even for the most alert, serious truth teller to recognize.

A simple example will demonstrate this point. In teaching classes and seminars, and just in personal conversations, I have found a little exercise quite revealing. I first select an individual to dialogue with me in an exchange that goes like this:

"Melissa, have you ever lied?" I begin.

Practically everyone I ask responds aloud, "Sure I have lied. Everybody has."

Then I proceed by saying, "If someone were to ask me, 'Do you know Melissa R____?' and I reply, 'Yes, I know Melissa,' and then the inquirer asks, 'What can you tell me about her?' would I be telling the truth if I said, 'She is an admitted liar'?"

Most initial responses are an embarrassing, "Yes, that is the truth. She did admit it." At the same time, nearly everyone feels uncomfortable with this label— particularly Melissa. Discussion leads some to reaffirm that my comment about

Melissa was technically true, but that I shouldn't say such a thing. Others assert that I would not be telling the truth but cannot specifically identify why my comment would be a lie.

For the record, let me register here that if I said, "Melissa is an admitted liar," I would be lying. Why this statement is a lie will be made clear in the next few paragraphs.

■ "THE PLAIN FACTS" ARE NOT ENOUGH

If "the facts" are not enough to measure truth telling, what definition of truth can we use to guide ourselves and condemn the crafty schemers and scammers?

I cite here the best definition of honesty I know. It was given by Robert Louis Stevenson in a short essay entitled "Truth of Intercourse" (a discussion of social relationships). *"To tell the truth, rightly understood, is not just to state the true facts, but to convey a true impression."*[2] In other words, when I fail to convey a true impression, by whatever means, I am lying.

I am sure that with a little thought, nearly everyone can recall an incident in which strict adherence to facts still conveyed a dishonest and untruthful message. Like the disappointed purchaser of a used car pointing to the large sign, "Guaranteed Used Cars" and the car lot manager saying, "But we do guarantee that they are used," it is possible to stick to the facts but still lead someone to believe something very different from the truth.

For instance, consider the statements, "Well, isn't that a masterpiece?" or "Isn't she a beauty?" or "Boy, isn't he fast?" These phrases can be understood to either be complimentary or, with a different inflection in the voice, convey criticism or sarcasm.

Referring back to the conversation with Melissa, the words "she's an admitted liar" are factually sticking very close to the words from her mouth. How honest (exact) can one be, actually quoting another person? She did admit to lying. Then why, with all that attention to factual exactness, would I be lying about Melissa? Because to the typical listener, the phrase "she's an admitted liar" conveys the impression that Melissa is worse about telling the truth than the average person. Nothing we have heard from her indicates she is worse than anyone else—"everybody has lied." The word "liar" in our society, is a severe negative. It carries extra meaning and nuance. Prefixing the word "liar" with "admitted" to describe Melissa, is a grave distortion—a lie—because it does not convey a true impression. And look at the devastation this subtle use of words could cause as a character reference for Melissa. In interpersonal relationships, words often carry additional or different meanings than indicated by a dictionary or the law. Sadly, in the world of business, these subtleties of language are often used to mislead, deceive, or ensnare potential clients, investors, customers, competitors, and others. The next chapter will provide many specifics about the ways we lie.

◼ SINCERITY IS NOT ENOUGH

Some people attempt to reassure that they are truth tellers by saying, "But I really do believe this is the best product," or "I really didn't believe we had a deal." This leads us to the question, "Can we be truly sincere in what we say and still convey a falsehood?" If we say, "The world is flat," and we really believe it, does sincerity make the statement true? Isn't the statement still false—a lie? So enthusiastic believers must always search their own consciences if they really want to merit the label "an honest person." To consistently ensure that we are telling the truth, we must earnestly ask ourselves questions such as, "Is this conveying a true impression?", "Should I ask more questions before declaring it the truth?," and "Should I indicate that this is only my belief or opinion so others do not accept it as the absolute truth?," "Should I emphasize the negatives a little more so people do not draw the wrong conclusion?" The implications of this concept, that sincerity is not enough, are explored further in Chapter Six.

The idea that truth has not been told until the correct impression is conveyed may, for many, seem to be a very high—or even impossible— standard. Perhaps this is so. On the other hand, whether it is achievable or not, it sets a standard by which we can measure our words and behavior. Without such a common standard for honesty, for

GET RICH QUICK

I recently heard a similar deception in a radio advertisement. An announcer in a standard 60-second spot encouraged people to invest in an investment commodities plan wherein, "If you only invest $10,000 or $15,000 now, your investment is projected to grow to $100,000 to $200,000 over the next three to five years." The advertisement urged its listeners to call toll-free to take advantage of this great opportunity. During almost the entire ad, an enthusiastic voice proclaimed how great the returns *could* be, implying to the listener, *"would* be." But near the end, one short sentence was inserted in a very quick, subdued voice, saying, "Investors should be aware that they could lose their entire principal." This was followed by another reassuring statement of how great this opportunity was to get rich.

Was this a truthful message? Technically, yes. Did it convey a true impression? Not to me. It conveyed the impression that there was a 90 percent chance you could get rich and a small 10 percent chance you could lose all your money. In my experience, the odds of getting rich in such investment schemes for the lay person are 50–50 at best, and often much worse.

Many people are unaware when they are being untruthful. Let's look at one common business practice in light of our definition, which requires us to convey a true impression.

How often do you see items on display in a store priced at $1.00, $20.00, $100.00, or $20,000.00, or some other number rounded to the nearest dollar? Most often, we see prices such as $.99, $19.99, $99.99, or $19,995.00—we even see gasoline priced at $1.19 and $^9/_{10}$. Why is this? Is this because in adding up and calculating taxes the 9s are easier to handle than the 0s? Why do we tolerate this cumbersome number system? Surely when we buy gasoline, the actual difference between $1.19 and $^9/_{10}$ and $1.20 amounts to maybe one or two pennies per tank at the most and does not justify the complications of all those 9s.

We use this deception because it works. Otherwise, we would quickly go for the more efficient and convenient system of zeros. Marketers know that most people tend to look only at the first digits in a number when they are making a decision based on price. Emotionally, consumers feel that $19.99 is closer to $19.00 than it is to $20.00. The method conveys the impression that $.99 is significantly less than $1.00, and people are led to believe that they are paying less, or at least not more, than the rounded amount.

judging and debating, the air can get filled with charges and countercharges—accusations of dishonesty and claims of honesty that seldom lead to fruitful dialogue. But with an agreed-upon standard, we can transform accusations into building blocks of understanding. When someone says, "I told the truth," and another person argues, "It was a lie," a debate may follow. But if the second person asks instead if the first person conveyed a true impression, the question can often bring the discussion into focus.

An agreed-upon working definition of truth telling can serve as an important bridge to understanding. Without such a definition, claims and accusations can be flung endlessly back and forth, seldom resulting in better or more effective interpersonal or group relationships. For those who don't like my proposed definition, create one of your own, but do get a working definition. Anyone aspiring to be a person of integrity must have a working definition of truth. Without it, most discussions of honesty become just talk.

Would you like to test the idea? Think of the last time you or a member of your family saw the price of gasoline on a sign that said "$1.59 $^9/_{10}$" but actually reported it as "$1.60." Most people would report it as "$1.59," wouldn't they? Merchants gain almost one additional penny on each gallon of gas without the customer feeling the pain of an additional penny, an additional dollar or more on any product without any additional customer discomfort.

Some people counter that the method is truthful: all the facts are there—all the little 9s. No one is getting ripped off, right? "Is it my fault if people don't pay attention to the little things?" you may ask yourself. But remember, truth telling means conveying a true impression, not just stating the facts.

Some may scoff that this example is such a little matter. But I am trying to establish the subtle and delicate nature of truth, and this is one of the best visual examples I can find. Gross lying usually begins with small things like this and grows into progressively more vicious lies, and then people wonder how it came to be. Small matters like pricing create the fertile environment that nourishes creative people in a competitive climate to grow small, questionable behaviors into blatant lies, letter by letter, syllable by syllable, word by word, and sentence by sentence, without ever becoming aware of it.

In a highly competitive world, honesty does not come naturally. Conveying a true impression to avoid stepping over the line can be an awesome challenge. I was raised with the impression that truth was bold, bright, shining, and readily recognized by almost everyone, and that lying was dark, dirty, dank, sinister, and easily recognized by regular people. This is just not so.

When my family lived in Africa, we were warned to always take a flashlight with us when we went out at night so we could see the snakes. At first, whenever we went out, we had our eyes peeled for large spitting cobras, puff adders, and black or green mambas—all deadly snakes. The small ones did not merit our attention because they looked more like worms. Finally, one day we became aware that the little worm-size snakes were just as deadly, if not more so. Our unawareness and inattention could have wreaked deadly results on my wife and me and our children.

So it is with truth and lying. They are not bright and bold or black and dirty. The truth is not always easily recognizable. An important second key in affirming our individual standards of honesty and establishing an environment of integrity in business is to be aware of the subtle, delicate, and fragile nature of truth: it must be handled with great skill, dexterity, and constant vigilance. The simplest things—tone of voice, facial expressions, or even slight pauses—can destroy truth. Imagine how the delicate truth must suffer among the flailing elbows and knees and the pushing and shoving of the competitive world, along with the constant pressure of self-interest to step over ethical and legal lines.

We should ask ourselves things like, "Did I convey a true impression to the boss in my last report?", "Did the company's annual report convey a true impression to the stockholders?", "Did I convey a true impression to that client about the risk of this investment in both my sales pitch and my advertisement?", and "Did I convey a true impression to my competitor about why I wanted the information I was seeking?"

I do not expect every businessperson to become completely truthful overnight. But I believe that just raising the issue will nudge you and the people in your organization to reach a more noble level of honesty rather than just ignore the issue. A working definition of truth is foundational to creating an institution of integrity.

CASE: A BANK WITH A HISTORY

Security Financial Bank commenced business in 1908 and had over two decades of financial prosperity. Then, as happened to many other banks, the Great Depression took a heavy toll, eventually causing the bank to declare bankruptcy and close its doors in late 1932.

In 1952, Theodore Sebastian launched his own banking enterprise. As he tried to come up with an attractive name for his company, he came across the records of Security Financial Bank and learned of its demise. After much research and investigation, he legally obtained the right to use that name, and later that year, he opened his new financial institution.

Knowing how important trust, reliability, and security would be in the banking business, he wanted to convey an image of stability. The building's architecture and interior decorations conveyed a feeling of solid strength and financial prosperity. Sebastian knew that length of time in continuous operation would also convey a sense of stability. A sign on the front of the building read, "Security Financial Bank—Founded in 1908." The same message appeared on the bank's letterhead and in all its advertisements. After the bank began to grow, other branches were opened, and each of them had the same sign out front: "Founded in 1908."

QUESTIONS

1. Was the owner of the bank dishonest or deceitful? If so, was this just a small inconsequential matter?

2. Are the banker's actions the first step down the slippery slope to blatant lying and fraud? Would you trust this banker if you knew what he had done to obtain the name on his bank or place "Founded in 1908" on his sign?

3. Is stretching your age by a year or padding your résumé an unimportant matter?

CHAPTER THREE

Avoiding Deception

FOR A LONG TIME, one of Tylenol's advertisements headlined, "WHY DOCTORS REC-OMMEND TYLENOL MORE THAN ALL LEADING ASPIRIN BRANDS COMBINED." The copy went on to tell how "Tylenol is safer than aspirin" and "just as effective."[1]

What is the message of this advertisement? Most people understood this to mean that doctors recommended Tylenol more than aspirin, that Tylenol is safe while aspirin is not always safe. Tylenol does everything aspirin can do. Is this honest advertising or a case of deception?

The makers of Tylenol were trying to capitalize on what is known as the "bandwagon" effect: everybody's doing it. In their advertisement, they claimed that most doctors think Tylenol is best. So based on the working definition of truth telling presented in the previous chapter—to tell the truth is not just to state the facts, but to convey a true impression—did the Tylenol advertisement convey a true impression? What impression did the advertisers intend to convey? If the advertisement did not convey a true impression, then it must have been deceptive—possibly even fraudulent.

Executives at Bayer, a major aspirin manufacturer, recognized the ad as deceitful. In an advertisement designed to attack and expose Tylenol's dishonest ad campaign, Bayer blasted, "Makers of Tylenol, shame on you!"

Although Bayer acknowledged that Tylenol's statement "Doctors recommend Tylenol more than all leading aspirin brands combined" was technically correct, it pointed out, "Just think how many times doctors say, 'take aspirin' without mentioning a specific brand." According to Bayer, the real truth was that "Doctors recommend aspirin more than twice as often as they recommend Tylenol."[2]

It appears, based on our definition, that Tylenol engaged in deceptive advertising. Ostensibly, the ad was designed to lead people to believe that doctors recommend Tylenol more than aspirin, when in fact, doctors recommend aspirin twice as often as Tylenol. Tylenol (or the Tylenol company) launched a campaign "to cause people to accept as true or valid that which is false or invalid,"[3] which is by definition, deception.

Bayer also pointed out that Tylenol's claim to being safe was misleading because "leading medical experts have expressed great concern about the occurrence of liver damage with acetaminophen" (an ingredient in all Tylenol products). In addition, Bayer stated that Tylenol's claim to being "just as effective" as aspirin was also deceptive, as "inflammation can be a major cause of pain, and Tylenol does nothing about inflammation—absolutely nothing."[4] Therefore, we can conclude that Tylenol was lying.

But that sounds so harsh. Surely, we reason, it wasn't that bad. Here is an example of Key #1, where we are tempted to avoid calling a spade a spade, and thus allow our self-deception to keep us from taking the needed action toward creating an institution of integrity.

■ FOUR SUBTLE TOOLS OF DECEPTION

Most forms of deception are centered around manipulations of the communication process. This is done in four basic ways:

1) Stating things that are not so—outright lying.
2) Overstating or exaggerating a situation or condition.
3) Understating circumstances.
4) Withholding information.

While each of these tools can be used separately, they are frequently used in combination as in the Tylenol incident.

The first major tool of deception, stating things that are not so, is regarded as blatant lying and is commonly accepted as dishonest. Many think of this as the only way people lie; if you avoid saying anything obviously false, you can claim to be an honest person. Examples of blatant lying are stating that a parcel of land has water rights when there are none, saying a check is in the mail when it is still sitting on the desk, claiming you have no knowledge of an action when just yesterday you participated in a meeting about it, insisting that you have never been convicted of a felony when you have, or writing a résumé that shows a college degree when you never enrolled in college.

The ad stating that Tylenol is "just as effective" as aspirin—when aspirin treats inflammation, a major cause of pain, and Tylenol does absolutely nothing for inflammation—is one of those direct falsehoods.

Other whoppers:

1872:   Standard Oil's John D. Rockefeller conspires with the railroads to handicap his competitors through the South Improvement Company. Under oath he lies about his ties to the organization.

1999:   Madison Square Garden's Dave Checketts denies meeting Phil Jackson to discuss a New York Knicks coaching job. Later he apologizes for lying.

1999:   Jeff Papows, president of Lotus, is accused of telling tall tales about his past. Among other things, Papows wasn't orphaned, didn't earn a Ph.D. from Pepperdine, and didn't eject from a plane while training for the Gulf War.[5]

Even though most of us recognize that saying things that are not true is outright lying, many still engage in this type of dishonesty. Often, the lies are told in an effort to avoid trouble, get out of a tight spot, gain a sale and, avoid embarrassment or being caught in wrongdoing. This phenomenon is explored in Chapter Six when the effects of pressure are discussed.

■   OVERSTATING OR EXAGGERATION

Direct lying is not the only way a person besmirches his or her integrity. The incident of the bank being advertised as "FDIC approved," in the previous chapter, shows how the ever-so-subtle use of language can grossly misrepresent. Some people become unusually skillful in developing the art of deception in the subtlest of ways—often with very serious consequences. Overstatement and exaggeration can create falsehoods as great as outright lying.

The great persuaders in our society—who include people who make their living in sales, marketing, advertising, public relations, journalism, politics, law, and religion—are quite prone to develop and use the art of exaggeration. When selling an item or promoting a cause, persuaders have a tendency to embellish the benefits of the things they are espousing, as well as the negative aspects of competitive products or causes.

Several years ago, advertising for IRA accounts among banks in Maryland demonstrated the deception often employed in the practice of overstatement and exaggeration. Newspaper advertisements placed by local banks contained two important features: the "bonus rate" placed in very large print, and the regular base rate printed at one fraction the size of the bonus rate. One bank advertised:

25% BONUS RATE FOR TWO MONTHS.

10.87% AFTER APRIL 16 ANNUAL COMPOUNDING.

Another bank advertised a 15 percent bonus rate for two months, accompanied by a regular rate of 11.5 percent for twenty-eight months. Both banks' large-print emphasis on the bonus rate, which was only available for two months, was an exaggeration that did not convey a true impression. Which should a person have selected? Twenty-five percent sure looked good compared to 15 percent. But the actual effective annual yields, which were never disclosed in the ads and which most people wouldn't have stopped to calculate, were quite different from the overstated bonus rates. Annual effective yields were actually 12.31 percent for the first bank (compared with a bonus rate of 25 percent) and 12.39 percent for the second bank (compared to a bonus rate of 15 percent).[6]

Not long ago, I received in the mail an 8 by 11-inch envelope with big declarations on the front and the back. The very bold print on the front immediately captured my attention:

AMERICAN EXPRESS CARD MEMBERS

PRIZE ELIGIBILITY NOTICE

WINNING NUMBERS HAVE BEEN SELECTED

QUINN G. MCKAY

(In red) GUARANTEED & BONDED SWEEPSTAKES

(address)

(at bottom) NO CASH AWARD LESS THAN $1,000.00

Inside, an official looking certificate with six "exclusive numbers" asked me to sign and indicate whether I preferred the "cash prize" or the "merchandise option." This, along with the multiple personal numbers, began to make me feel like maybe I had already won. Was I close to a slam dunk? The package also included eleven other pages of "information." The pages noted a grand prize of $1,666,675.00 and printed this specific figure ten different times. Prizes of $100,000 were mentioned eight times, and $25,000 nine times. The copy also told me that "hundreds more free prizes" were available. "No prize less than $1,000—over 10,000 prizes yet to be awarded totaling $1,937,675.00." So many $ signs. I felt money was just floating everywhere.

After going through the material, it appeared to me that I had a good chance of winning something. A very reputable company name, "American Express," was the first thing to greet me. The inside pages verified that this was sponsored by the "American Express Publishing House." The company personalized the document with my name, giving me an extra set of exclusive numbers for good luck, and promised that thousands of prizes would be awarded (including the grand prize worth over one million dollars and all other prizes worth at least $1,000 each). The word "Guaranteed" added further emotional reassurance. It wasn't a slam dunk, I reasoned, but it was surely worth the time to respond.

I should have been skeptical when I was confronted with a page and a half of text that described the joys of owning a subscription to *Travel and Leisure* magazine. But I suppose a trial subscription would have been a small price to pay for the chance to win such big prizes.

In the interest of research, I took the time to read another third of a page that I found on the back of the very last page of the packet in tiny print. The print was literally half the size of the print you are now reading. The section was titled, "Official Rules—No Purchase Necessary." I learned that of the 10,006 prizes available, 10,000 were worth only $10 each—not the $1,000 minimum amount I had read about earlier. I also discovered that I had only a one in 12,000 chance to win even $10, and that the odds of winning any one of the six big prizes were one in 120 million. Fat chance.

I was particularly disappointed, not because it was such a long shot to win, but because I had always held the sponsoring company in such high esteem. Now, for the most part, the company technically stated all the facts (except for telling me that every prize was worth at least $1,000 when 10,000 prizes were worth only $10), but by overstating the chances of winning, the company severely violated the truth by conveying the wrong impression.

Casual truth tellers argue, "but it was an honest promotion, all the 'facts' were there to read." If this were the case, why didn't the writers put on the front page in normal or bold type, "Your chances of winning one of the six large prizes is one in 120 million" rather than hiding it in tiny print on the back of the eleventh page? The answer to that is obvious: because that would make for a very poor sales piece; few would read beyond the first page. In Chapter Seven, I will explain how this type of gross deception has become acceptable in the world of business.

Ironically, if the CEO of American Express were challenged, he would most likely attest that his company takes great pride in its high standard of integrity.

What kind of message does this send to young people, employees, etc.? That shading the truth is okay? That deliberately misleading others is okay? After all, if a credible financial institution, among the Fortune 500, can manipulate the truth to its advantage, despite its formal and rigid ethical code, it must be acceptable, right?

Overstatements, often called puffery, are used widely to deceive not only in advertising, but also in selling, negotiating contracts, seeking leverage, and in many other activities—especially in the pressure of highly competitive circumstances. Jane Bryant Quinn accurately sums up the problems of exaggeration in business: "In the fight against the tendency of the overblown to overstep, nice guys finish last."[7]

The practice of exaggeration is not just a phenomenon of the past tense. Every few days, new revelations of exaggeration continue to surface, frequently in numbers enough to give strong evidence that it is a common practice in business.

The Business Section of 20 March, 2003, of one city's newspaper read:

SEC CHARGES HEALTHSOUTH WITH FRAUD
Rehabilitation giant and its chairman accused of overstating earning, by $1.4 billion.
'HealthSouth's standard operating procedure was to manipulate the com pany's earnings to create the false impression that the company was meeting Wall Street's expectations, " said Stephen Cutler, SEC Enforcement Director.

It is the habit, and maybe the right, of corporations and individuals to show their best face at every level of endeavor, not just in annual reports and financial statements but also in personal appearance in an employment interview. Does dying one's hair to look younger constitute an exaggeration of one's youth that is

Just how subtle can you get? Try the 1996 presidential campaign as reported in *U.S. News and World Report*. Along with citing "fudging facts," "withholding information," and similar devices, the writers state:

"'Deceptions are subtle,' says Wellesley College political scientist Marion Just. 'Candidates can be accurate in the most superficial ways and still be deceptive.'

"How? Words matter less than pictures. To judge from Clinton's ads, Bob Dole has never been photographed in color, a not-so-subtle reminder of his age. Black-and-white footage frequently twins Dole and Newt Gingrich, the unpopular House speaker. Dole ads use the same formula."[9]

Just the cleverness of one candidate always shown in color and the opponent always shown in black-and-white conveys an impressive message. Is it deceit?

in fact deception? Between that and an obvious lie of $1.4 billion, where does putting forth one's best face end and fraud begin?

Many small things can add up to gross misrepresentation as happened with HealthSouth. In a story about selecting a CEO for an Internet company and later finding out he had fudged on his résumé, *Business Week* stated, "What's one more? Surveys show that as many as one-third of job candidates embellish their résumés."[8]

For an institution that is concerned about integrity, frequent and continuing discussions *with examples* about where you draw the line in your organization are necessary.

■ UNDERSTATING CIRCUMSTANCES

The third device of deception, understatement, to some degree is simply the mirror image of exaggeration or overstatement. In the Tylenol ad, by implication they significantly understated the relative number of times doctors prescribe aspirin over Tylenol. It is such a common practice it deserves its own page. How often when something goes wrong do people say, "I was not at that meeting," "that was not my responsibility," or "that was really out of my hands."

An interesting public example was the Salt Lake City Winter Olympics. Some time after the city had won the vote of the International Olympic Committee to host the 2002 Winter Olympics, a major scandal broke out. The Salt Lake Organizing Committee was accused of "buying votes," specifically by—against Olympic rules—wining, dining, entertaining, and giving free surgery for voting delegates, as well as providing college expenses and free junkets to the United States for their family members.

Obviously, members of the board and many other people were not only aware of what was going on but were also participants in delivering the perks. However, when the charges became public, not one member of the board came forward publicly or privately to admit they knew a thing about the activity. One prominent member of the board was heard to say, "I'm so mad the staff would do that and cloud my reputation." Though there was evidence that specific entertainment activities had been discussed in the board meetings, when the CEO and CFO were accused of wrongdoing, not one board member came forward to say, "Yes, I had a part in these activities." They either denied that they had been aware of it, or just kept silent. The two officers were indicted, spending months and months and thousands of dollars defending themselves without any of their associates coming to their defense.

This incident is raised as an example of a very frequent activity that causes so many of us to lie by understatement. To test the idea and challenge your level of integrity, watch for the next time something goes embarrassingly wrong and see how easy it is for you to step forward and say, "Maybe I had some responsibility," or "You know, that was really my fault." For most people, the tendency and initial reaction is to minimize our roles of responsibility. Don't fool yourself by citing an incident when there was little at stake or that was just a small faux pas as an example of its being easy to step forward with full acknowledgments. Pick an incident where something big is at stake—like your reputation—and see how easy it is then to be forthright.

Sometimes good wordsmiths can use language to gloss over or understate the negative aspects of a situation. Spin doctors are professionals at this task, especially in a political setting.

An example of the art of clever understatement is found in a story about Winston Churchill that I was told while I lived in England. Churchill had been speaking for several minutes, giving a speech as a young parliamentarian, when some of his opponents began to openly accuse him of lying. Throughout the remainder of the afternoon, Churchill adamantly denied that he had lied, but his opponents just as adamantly continued to accuse him.

At the beginning of the next day's session, Churchill arose and asked the prime minister if he could address the Parliament as a matter of personal privilege. After he was granted the chance to speak, Churchill is reported to have addressed his fellow parliamentarians by saying, "I would like to assure this august body that this member does not lie. He did not lie yesterday, he does not lie today, nor will he lie tomorrow. He does, however, arise on this occasion to acknowledge that yesterday he did indulge in a terminological inexactitude." Surely that does not sound as audacious as lying, but it describes the same thing.

"A retired superintendent of Utah's Dinosaur National Monument [Denny

Huffman] released internal National Park Service memos Wednesday, [17 March 2004] that coached park bosses on ways to hide the true nature of Bush administration cutbacks on park services from the public.

"Huffman . . . released a February 20, 2004 e-mail to park superintendents in the northeastern United States that outlined potentially controversial cuts by Park Service Deputy Randy Jones. Among the cutbacks: reducing the number of life guards on beaches, eliminating all ranger-guided tours, not cutting lawns, privatizing campgrounds, and closing parks every Sunday and Monday [this summer season]. "The memo told superintendents to refrain from issuing news releases about the cuts.

"He [Jones] suggested that if you feel you must inform the public through a press release on this year's hours or day of operation, for example, that you state what the parks' plans are and not directly indicate that 'this is a cut in comparison to last year's operation' reads the e-mail, apparently written by Northeastern Deputy Regional Director Sandy Walters. If pressed 'use the terminology of service level adjustment due to fiscal constraints' to describe the cuts, the memo said.

"The previous December, U.S. Park Police Chief Teresa Chambers had been ousted after she told media outlets budget cuts had forced a reduction of patrols around Washington area monuments." (Christopher Smith, "Department Memo Told Park Heads to Spin Cuts," the *Salt Lake Tribune*, Salt Lake City, UT 18 March 2004: p. C2)

Examples of the subtlety and cunning of dishonest understatements are many. Look at advertisements for tobacco. Though every year more than 400,000 people in the United States die prematurely of tobacco-related diseases, most of the ads for these products show pictures of attractive, vigorous, healthy young people. Casual truth tellers maintain there is an explicit warning label on advertisements. Serious truth tellers recognize

---

Bill Goebels proudly whisked his new car up to the gas station. Station attendant Harry Smith admired it as he filled the tank.

"It's a lovely car," Harry remarked, "and you were smart to get rid of that other heap before the transmission went out on you. Like I told you last time I worked on it, it might've lasted one more day if you were lucky. Did they catch it at the agency?"

"No. I got a nice trade-in on it. The sales manager just looked at the rubber on it, took a good look inside, said it looked like a real clean car, and made me a nice offer—no questions asked. I guess he really wanted to make a sale. I'd hate to be the guy who buys that jalopy, but I figured it wasn't up to me to teach that character at the agency his business. If I'd been dealing directly with a private customer, it might have been different. Anyway, the transmission may still last for a while. Besides, nobody else gave me a break like that."[10]

Is Bill Goebels acting with honesty? Did Bill Goebels lie? If the salesman at the agency sells the car to a customer without mentioning the condition of the transmission, is he dishonest? Even if he didn't know? Is ignorance or a claim of ignorance a valid excuse for a person of integrity?

---

that the whole ad conveys that tobacco is not such a big health risk after all. If a picture is worth a thousand words, the picture of a beautiful person surely outweighs a dozen words on a label warning of health risks.

■ **WITHHOLDING INFORMATION**

In some ways, the fourth tool of deception, withholding information, has become the most accepted, apparently because many people are not aware that it is a form of deceit. But most people are aware that in a court of law, if an attorney is aware of important and relevant information in a case and fails to disclose it to the court, the case may be dismissed or the attorney may be held in contempt of court, and that contracts can be invalidated if one of the parties learns that important information was deliberately withheld that would have changed the terms of the contract or that would have influenced the party to not sign. For those concerned about integrity, the tricky challenge is determining guidelines as to what is "important" and what is not. Withholding information is almost always a key factor in fraud. At one time or another, nearly everyone has been offended or deceived by someone who withheld essential information.

In the past, horse traders developed reputations for not only failing to reveal that their horse balked or had respiratory problems, but also for going to great lengths to cover up defects and prevent prospective buyers from discovering problems until after the sale had been made.

Today, persuaders and defenders alike engage in the practice of withholding information. Salespeople who deliberately point out a product's defects or who let their customers know that the products can be purchased elsewhere at a lower price won't likely win sales rep of the year or endear themselves to their employers. If executives at Tylenol had proposed that the company's advertisement plainly state that liver damage might arise from the ingestion of one of Tylenol's ingredients, or that the product doesn't treat inflammation, a major cause of pain, the comments would undoubtedly have been frowned upon. Legally, it is the primary responsibility of the buyer to find out the adverse aspects of a deal, and it is not the responsibility of the seller to volunteer the information; thus, *caveat emptor*, "let the buyer beware," still plays an important role in business activities.

Michael Deaver, an assistant to President Ronald Reagan, explained that in public relations, the practice of withholding strategic information is helpful for maintaining a good public image. He said, "When you're talking to the media, be a well, not a fountain."[11] Incidents such as the famous leak at the Three Mile Island nuclear power plant, have often caused me to wonder how the presidents of these organizations react to such a crisis. Do they immediately call in the public relations team and say, "Now whatever you do, be honest with the public. Don't deliberately withhold information from them."? It seems that many organizations will go to great lengths to assess how much bad news they can suppress without negative consequences.

On the other hand, many people would rightly argue that for the good of the company, the employees, or the public, it is sometimes necessary to withhold information. The withholding of information is acknowledged as a common and acceptable practice, suggesting that in the game of business there are times when deception is all right. So when is deception by withholding information acceptable, and when is it not? When people—especially executives—fail to establish proper guidelines and live by them, it is necessary to enact such legislation as the Truth in Lending Act, the Truth in Advertising Act, and so forth.

Withholding information is a tool of deception frequently exercised by people who find themselves in the position of either "persuader" or "defender." Those who desire to maintain their character and honesty when engaged in such roles should be doubly cautious of the temptation to withhold information. Any organization that wants to be noted for its integrity must pay careful and extensive attention to the challenges and temptations of withholding information.

Another form of withholding information is what is commonly called "low-balling." Tom L. Beauchamp, explains that this technique always involves withholding information in a more or less "intentionally ordered interaction":

This tactic [low-balling] typically involves revealing certain less favorable or unfavorable aspects of an agreement to a person only after the person has already made an *initial* decision to perform some action . . . [but] unlike most ordinary uses of withholding to deceive and manipulate, in low-balling the withheld information is revealed to the manipulee before the manipulee makes an *irrevocable* commitment by, for example, actually signing a sales agreement. . . . [In] a case from retail sales: A salesperson is concluding negotiations with a customer for the purchase of a set of automobile tires. After the sales clerk has written up the first half of the receipt and has [the customer's] credit card in hand, he observes that the $150 price does not include three forms of tax, and then casually mentions that charges for mounting the tires and balancing the wheels are extra, as is the cost of an extended warranty policy that is highly recommended for these tires. The total charge for all goods and services, including sales tax, is $202.50. The clerk asks if the customer still wants the tires, and if so, which of the additional services is desired. Meanwhile, the clerk is poised to complete the receipt and credit card form.[12]

Thus, "low-balling" involves withholding information until an initial decision or tentative commitment has already been made.

■ THE COVER-UP

A cover-up is defined as "a device or stratagem for masking or concealing." Ever since Watergate, the cover-up has become a synonym for dishonesty at the top. But although most people imagine cover-ups to be limited to top political figures or powerful corporate officers who have committed some massive dastardly deed and now want to suppress all knowledge of it, cover-ups are actually so common they are practiced—in a major or minor way—almost universally.

Cover-ups employ all four tools of deception, and are undertaken regularly by people in the most respected ranks and the lowliest. The pressure to engage in a cover-up is often intense, and often spawns from noble objectives such as the desire to be loyal, as seemed to be the case with junior Nixon administration aides in the early 1970s. Other motivations also drive people to cover up: fear of reprisal, fear of loss, and most commonly, fear of embarrassment. When people are caught in a mistake or ethical blunder, or when they are caught doing something they know is wrong, it seems almost innately human to react with a cover-up: They either state something that is not so, understate their role in the matter, or withhold information that would confirm their guilt.

The Francis Gary Powers U2 spy plane incident over Russia is one of the best-known and most blatant attempts at cover-up. During Dwight D. Eisenhower's presidency, the Russians announced that they had shot down a U.S. spy plane over their country. Eisenhower adamantly proclaimed to the public that no such thing could have taken place because the United States had no spy planes over Russia. Of course, admitting to the illegal flights would have been a public embarrassment. When the Russians finally presented the evidence, a very red-faced administration was forced to admit that the illegal espionage flights had been carried out deliberately over an extended period of time.

Washington, D.C. is certainly a hotbed of cover-ups—just consider how many

Another form of cover-up was discussed in an article in the *Wall Street Journal* in 1983, about the controversial practice of off-balance-sheet financing—an accounting tactic designed to hide corporate debt from unaware bankers and investors to enhance borrowing power.

Consider Avis Rent-A-Car, a subsidiary of Norton Simon, Inc. In 1980, Avis set up a trust to borrow money to buy automobiles, which it then leases to Avis for its rental fleet. Because the trust is separate from Avis and Norton Simon, the trust's debt is not on their balance sheets. The result: Norton Simon kept $400 million in borrowings off its balance sheet for the year ended June 30. Robert D. Walter, Norton Simon's principal accounting officer, says the trust arrangement held Norton Simon's debt down to 56 percent of equity at June 30, rather than the 140 percent that it otherwise would have been.

One of the big advantages of off-balance-sheet financing, Mr. Walters concedes, is that "it

(continued on next page)

legal investigations are being carried out by the Justice Department, or how many congressional committees are engaged almost full-time in trying to find out what the executive branch or a member of Congress is withholding from them. But government officials by no means have an exclusive claim on them.

Cover-ups are carried out by most people at one time or another. If you hope to maintain a business with a reputation for integrity, this is one area that will need your special attention. Otherwise, things could get out of hand, just as they have for many people in the past. After all, cover-ups are only undertaken when people feel that damage to their reputations could be severe. But because the news of a cover-up is doubly devastating, it is necessary to cover up the cover-ups too, right? Of course, for those whose philosophy embraces bluffing or "gaming ethics," this is just another part of the game, and the more skilled one becomes at covering up, the more successful that person will be in the games of big business and politics.

■ THE RIGHT TO PRIVACY AND THE RIGHT TO KNOW

Amid all this finger-pointing and exploration of withholding information, there is a challenging concept that requires rigorous thought: the right to privacy. This idea holds that institutions and individuals have the right to keep some things just to themselves. That is, they can keep from the knowledge of others certain thoughts, feelings, actions, plans, and behaviors and still have a legitimate claim to a reputation of integrity.

This concept is worthy of an entire book by itself, to develop useful concepts, principles, rules, and guidelines to govern what information is appropriately kept private and what must be revealed. Some may be obvious; a company's name and address, corporate officers' names, and financial reports should be generally available. Other information like formulas, special production systems, sources of special materials, information considered proprietary (such as research) or an individual's personal thoughts and feelings, are legitimately private.

However, there is a great host of items that are in dispute or up for question. Some information the holder may regard as private, but the seeker may regard as part of his or her right to know. For instance, a company intends to merge with another company. Not only does the question arise, "Is it legitimate to keep this concealed," but also "Who has the right to know?" Employees? Investors? City officers? Banks? In addition, when is the ethical *time* to share the information to avoid a cover-up and still not disrupt negotiations that are in progress?

permits us to make other borrowings from banks for operating capital that we couldn't otherwise obtain." He adds that Norton Simon didn't give details of the trust in its annual report because that would have required a report "as thick as a Sears Roebuck catalog."

However, Gerry White, a securities analyst who teaches financial analysis at New York University, calls the tactic a "subterfuge." Avis, he says, isn't leasing the cars but really owns them."[13]

Coupling this 1983 incident with what has been revealed in the 2001–2003 business scandals gives evidence that these deceptive practices have been common behavior of even well-known companies for a long period of time.

■ HONESTY VS. PROMOTION

Most fraud is carried out by withholding select information, not by blatantly misstating the facts. In fact, we might ask: If exaggeration, understatement, and withholding information are forms of lying, how can anyone be a great salesperson, promoter, or campaigner, and still be an honest person? Answer: Perhaps no one can do both. But since our economic, political, and religious institutions are so reliant on promotion and salesmanship, what can we do to maintain those institutions and still promote a moral and honest society?

First, we can begin by acknowledging that many of our common practices really are dishonest. Until this honesty with ourselves takes place, not much progress toward becoming a more moral society will ever take place. As long as we continue to justify ourselves, make excuses, or rationalize that lying is not lying, nothing will change.

Second, we can apply one of two different strategies to address the problem: (1) We can begin to teach that, yes, lying is, or at least may be, sometimes the right thing for an honest person to do, and we can devise a new definition of truth telling—one that never requires us to convey a true impression, but only requires that we say truthful things, however clever and crafty those things may be. Then we can argue that, in marketing, advertising, selling, and other noble cover-ups for good causes, certain forms of lying are justified, or at least permitted. We can then standardize our "real-world" curriculum to engrain in our younger generations that, indeed, buyers must beware—*caveat emptor*. And, like the Romans of ancient times, our children will be less susceptible to the con artist and the clever sales pitch, knowing that only the ignorant fall prey to such petty devices; even if we find it justifiable to lie to others, at a minimum we can be honest with ourselves.

Or, (2) we can go in the opposite direction and establish heavy penalties for those who use any of the tools of deception, and substantial incentives for people or businesses that can establish a reputation for rigid honesty, warts and all.

Of course, both of these approaches have problems. The first one seems much too liberal for a culture that stresses "always be honest," despite the fact that we already live and breathe this strategy in our minds as a general rule. The second one seems far too Puritan, and may even require some kind of "big brother" technology and euphemistic political correctness that we, as a nation, claim to detest. In fact, many honest citizens already shop and vote based on their judgment of honesty, many businesspeople make an excellent living by maintaining their reputation for honesty, and political correctness and "watchdog" technology have certainly left their mark on twentieth-century culture. The balance lies somewhere between crass manipulation of others and self-righteous hypocrisy.

CASE: FIRE INSURANCE[14]

Oswald Meyer owned and operated a large and flourishing waste-paper and scrap-metal business. He had recently renewed his fire insurance on both of his warehouses. At the time, his agent, with whom he had been doing business for years, told him he could substantially reduce his insurance premiums by installing a rather expensive electrical precautionary appliance that had recently appeared on the market. Meyer promised to install the device within a week, and his agent completed the insurance renewal forms including the lower premium. Meyer fully intended to make the installation promptly, as he had promised, but the press of other business caused him to forget. The agent, who always had known Oswald Meyer to be a man of his word, thought no more about the matter.

Within a month, a fire completely destroyed the paper warehouse. Meyer suddenly remembered his promise to install the electrical appliance, and thought with horror of the crippling loss he could suffer if he failed to collect on the insurance. From the look of the damage, it seemed clear that the fire would have started and spread whether the electrical appliance had been installed or not. And, because of his long friendship with the insurance agent, Meyer was sure that the inspection would be rather perfunctory and that he would collect in full on the insurance policy if he simply kept quiet. Further, he reasoned, he had been paying high premiums for years, and this was his first fire.

QUESTIONS

1. What would you have done in Oswald Meyer's place? What should he do? Why?

2. If he shares the information with the agent, what should the agent do?

3. If the insurance company found out about the case, what do you think it would do? How should Meyer respond to the insurance company's action?

4. Was the insurance agent acting honestly when he signed up Meyer before the changes were made?

CHAPTER FOUR

Pressure Affects Honesty

"One day I was sitting at my desk located in one of the cubicles in the back office of the small accounting firm I had been working at for a few short months. One of the firm partners, Mr. Morris, came to me with a request. He asked me, 'Marsha, will you please pick up line two and tell the person on the phone that I am out of my office and could you please take a message?'

"I gave the partner a somewhat startled and confused look, not quite sure what to make of his request. After all, we were both in the office and the partner knew who it was on the phone. Acknowledging my puzzlement, he continued, 'You see, I am not in *my* office, I am in *your* office. Therefore, since I am not in *my* office, you can tell them that and I can return this person's call at a later time!'

"It seemed strange to me that what Mr. Morris was doing was going out of his way to prevent me from having to lie. That it was okay for me to tell the person on the phone that Mr. Morris was not in his office since he actually got up out of his office, walked a few dozen feet into my cubicle, and stood there while I took the call.

"I picked up the telephone and did exactly as the firm partner requested."[1]

WAS MARSHA ACTING IN HONESTY? Did she do the right thing? Was Mr. Morris being honest? While many see this incident as just a small matter—only a little white lie—it illustrates at least five concepts that may challenge workplace integrity, that may be encountered by you or your employees.

1) A working definition of honesty is necessary.

2) The first false steps are small steps.

3) Principles you or your company value may conflict with each other.

4) The pressure of a superior affects decisions.

5) The pressure of self-interest under competition affects decisions.

1. A working definition is necessary. Did Mr. Morris instruct Marsha to lie? With the definition outlined in the previous chapter, "convey a true impression," the obvious conclusion is that this was a lie, in spite of the technical sophistry of a few feet.

2. First false steps. Most cases of major deception, scamming, and fraud, begin with just small, almost innocent, steps. (We will discuss this and the next point further in the following chapter.)

3. Conflict of principle. This is a very interesting example of loyalty and honesty conflicting with each other.

4. Pressure of a superior. Marsha is a trained and active member of the U.S. Marine Corps, an institution that stresses honor as a supreme ideal. Add to this her personal values and the ethical code of the accounting profession, and you have a young woman with a well-established and reinforced standard of honesty. Even given this, however, when faced with the pressure of her superior's request, her personal standard gave way.

Research lends evidence to the idea that pressure from superiors can outweigh other factors in contributing to unethical behavior. A report from the American Management Association cites three different surveys spanning a twenty-year period; each survey identifies "behavior of superiors" as the number one factor in contributing to unethical behavior.[2] It's true, a superior's behavior was not the sole determinant, but it was the dominant factor.

Executives who think the key to creating a company of integrity is to just select "honest people" for employment, need to do some rethinking. Assuming that if you find an honest person you can count on them to always be honest is invalid. The climate of the environment in which they work and actual situations they confront can overpower personal traits of character. One article summed it up like this:

Almost half of the workers in a new survey admitted they had engaged in unethical or illegal acts in the past year because of workplace pressures.

Their most common misdeeds: cutting corners on quality control, covering

> "It's getting harder for the good kids to compete with the cheaters," reported Barbara Wood, director of competitive events at the Tulsa State Fair in March 1994. She was speaking of 4-H Club and Future Farmers of America livestock shows. According to Wood, "Youth livestock shows have been infiltrated by adult breeders who use these shows as marketing tools.
>
> "Apparently, some farmers and ranchers had become very creative in their marketing ability, producing animals almost exclusively for club show projects, and manipulating the kids, and driving this excessive competitiveness. They are cheating by altering the animals to be more attractive to the judges. This includes pumping steers with air or oil to fill out depressed areas on their bodies, feeding them steroids to bulk up their muscles, removing the ribs of lambs to make them appear to have longer loins, and gluing sawdust to the legs of steers to make the legs appear large or eliminate knock knees."[4]

up incidents, abusing or lying about sick days, lying to or misleading customers, and putting inappropriate pressure on others.

"Mid level managers reported the highest level of pressure to act unethically or illegally, which is not surprising given their large number of layoffs," said Edward F. Cunningham, president of Clark Associates in Uniondale, NY.[3]

People are particularly sensitive to the desires, wishes, and requests of their superiors—and rightly so: In most organizations an employee's superior has so much influence, if not control, over the worker's destiny—their pay, promotion, work assignments, recommendations for positions in the future, even whether employment will continue or not—that a worker ignores the desires of "the boss" at serious peril to their own well-being. This often-delicate superior/subordinate relationship can have such serious implications that it can make even slight pressure from a superior a major concern for a subordinate.

5. Pressure of self-interest under competition. The pressure to step over ethical and legal lines in our economic system is all pervasive. Nearly everyone crosses the lines at some time. Frequently, it's hard to tell whether a person jumped or was pushed. Sometimes the pressure is internal (arising from a worker's desires and needs—self-interest) and sometimes external (arising from the demands of the job, supervisor, or surrounding culture) or a combination of both. But the result is the same: unethical or illegal behavior.

The chart below diagrams the conflict between self-interest and ethics in an environment of competition.

This graph shows three categories of business practices: Area A represents actions that are both ethical and legal; Area B includes actions that may be unethical, but are still legal; and Area C shows actions that are both unethical and illegal. The shaded areas represent the additional alternative actions that can result in

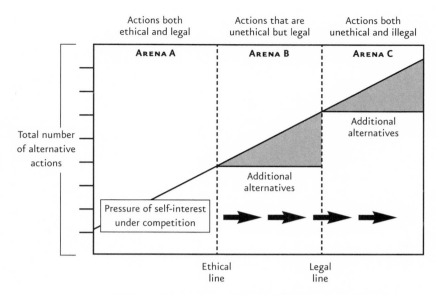

Actions both ethical and legal

Actions that are unethical but legal

Actions both unethical and illegal

SELF-INTEREST AND ETHICS UNDER COMPETITION

additional opportunities to people who decide to cross the "ethical" or "legal" lines. Such opportunities may represent increased income, improved status, or simply the unwillingness to "lose." The same shaded areas also represent the *perceived* risk to credibility or discipline. The *actual* risks to personal and organizational integrity and moral character begin at the ethical line.

The actions that fall in Areas A and C should be self-evident. Inherent in Area B is the idea that many actions that take place within the law or rules are, nonetheless, dishonest and unethical. For instance, those who maintain the Golden Rule as an ethical standard will be restrained from taking advantage of a customer's ignorance to make a sale, although it may be perfectly legal or within the rules to do so (remember *caveat emptor*—let the buyer beware). Telling a supplier that a check is "in the mail," while holding the check for a few more days for funds to arrive, may be legal, but it is hardly honest or ethical. At the Tulsa State Fair, mentioned on page 40, no law or rule specifically stated that pumping animals with air or oil, or feeding them steroids, was illegal. But it seems that the people in charge and the participants who didn't win the competition regarded those actions as highly unethical—"cheating." But having additional alternative actions available for use often gives a competitive advantage over those who act only in Area A.

Many businesspeople maintain a philosophy with no ethical lines, often without realizing it. Those who advocate that it's okay to take advantage of "all that the law or rules will allow," have done away with a separate ethical line. They do away with Area B and make the ethical and legal lines into one. To them everything that is legal is also ethical, and only illegal behavior is unethical. So, they claim, if there is no explicit rule against removing a lamb's rib to make it look better, then there is nothing wrong with doing so. This focuses concern on not crossing the legal line, and is the reason many corporations hire "compliance officers," sometimes called "ethical officers," whose main concern is not fairness or integrity but that the company doesn't get caught in violation of the law. Sometimes this concentration on legality will even push the line and decision makers will ask, "Can we get away with it legally?" or "Are we still within the law?"

In both theory and practice there is an "Area B" that represents actions that are legal but unethical. If this weren't the case, the word "ethical" would be redundant; *ethical* would be just a synonym for *legal*.

This is not a new concept. The idea that actions can be legal but unethical is widely held in American society. For instance, in paying taxes we are often told, "You would be a fool not to take advantage of all the law will allow." Ironically, those same people may feel it is wrong for athletes to take steroids—even if there is no rule against it. And even though there is no stated rule against gluing sawdust to a steer's legs, there is a sense, a feeling, that it is wrong. This is ethics: applied morality, often beyond what the law requires.

In fact, the fastest way to get a new law passed is for athletes, taxpayers, or business executives, to fail to act "ethically." Often, business executives only have themselves to blame for the burden of new laws and additional red tape. When they will not voluntarily refrain themselves or police others from pouring toxic waste into streams, they should not be surprised when a new law, with all its paperwork and inspections, gets passed declaring it illegal.

■ SELF-INTEREST PUSHES PEOPLE TO JUMP

Self-interest is the force that causes people to "jump" or be "pushed" over ethical and legal lines. It is like a prevailing wind that is so constant, persistent, and intense that the trees and shrubs in its path, a businessperson's moral and ethical standards, become permanently bent, their growth distorted by the pressure.

Understanding three characteristics of self-interest is helpful.

First, self-interest is *all pervasive*. It can be argued that all human actions are motivated by self-interest. With that logic, even acts of "charity" occur so the giver will feel better or assuage a guilty conscience or set a good example in groups that advocate charity. At any rate, no matter how good, honest, experienced, or capable you or your staff are, no one is exempt from self-interest, from the CEO to the sanitation crew.

SELF-INTEREST IS:

All-pervasive

Constant

Intense and Compelling

Second, self-interest is *constant*. It doesn't begin when you become a manager, and wouldn't end if you were fired. Whether it is exhibited for survival or to gain approval, recognition, or power, it is a persistent force.

Third, self-interest is often *intense and compelling*. People tend to work harder and longer hours when they see something in it for themselves. In most societies, money is the single best representation of what will satisfy most people's needs and wants. When a situation holds the possibility for a substantial financial reward, people are usually willing to invest great effort in terms of working, thinking, designing, and scheming.

So an economic system based on the opportunity for each individual to gratify a desire for money and all that money represents, is really capitalizing on the universal, constant, and often intense or compelling motivation of self-interest.

Why does this drive pressure us to cross ethical and legal lines? When we decide to stay well within Area A and avoid even the very appearance of unethical behavior, we commit ourselves to a serious disadvantage in a competitive system. How so?

People who are willing to play near the ethical line and even step over it increase the number of alternative actions available to them. This nearly always gives a competitive advantage. The more alternatives available, the greater the ability to compete. Further, people who not only step over the ethical line but also play right up against the legal line ("all the law will allow") in Area B have a great advantage over people who stay well back of the ethical line in Area A. Playing right up against the legal nearly always results in occasionally stepping *over* it just to grab one or two additional alternatives, giving a slight edge over competitors who are ignorant of the alternatives or who are unwilling to indulge in them. This is why the urge to step over the line can be strong in a competitive environment.

In business, that extra gift or entertainment, exaggeration of profits, or

OLYMPIC-SIZED SCANDAL

In June 1985, representatives from four U.S. cities were making bids to the U.S. Olympic Committee, hoping to be selected as the United States' nominee for the 1992 Winter Olympics. Anchorage, Alaska, won the decision over the three other cities: Lake Placid, Salt Lake City, and Reno/Lake Tahoe. A few days after the committee announced its decision, a Salt Lake City newspaper reported six lessons that the Salt Lake Winter Games Organizing Committee learned from the experience. Lesson two was "Olympic rules are apparently made to be broken."

"We were naïve," admitted one member of the Salt Lake committee. "We thought you played by the rules. The rules said 'no direct lobbying of U.S.O.C. [the United States Olympic Committee] members,' and we honored the rules. But we learned that Anchorage had a direct mailing go out to all U.S.O.C. members and that [Ted] Stevens, [a U.S. Senator from Alaska] contacted upwards of forty delegates."

Tom Welch, chairman of the Salt Lake committee said, "If we did one thing wrong, we followed the rules too closely. Anchorage and Lake Placid lobbied U.S.O.C. members directly—contrary to U.S.O.C. rules."[6]

Assuming that the number of reports in the news of people and companies overstepping ethical and legal lines is likely very small compared to the total number of incidents that actually occur, this tip-of-the-iceberg image suggests that overstepping is not uncommon, and more often than not, such actions go rewarded rather than punished.

dropped negative hint about a competing product, could make the difference in winning the contract or closing the sale.

In sports, the rewards for stepping over the ethical line can be great. One hundredth of a second can be the difference between a gold medal, with its glory and thousands of dollars in endorsements, and nothing. Doing steroids, blood doping, or taking cheap shots can be so tempting.

In a recent review of the fellowship applications of resident doctors, 29 percent of the applicants were found to have lied about their research, presentations, and articles. The reasons cited: "Intense competition," "Everyone is doing it," and "Why should I be at a disadvantage for being honest?"[5]

■ WINNING: THE NAME OF THE GAME

Deeply embedded in the American private enterprise culture is the obsession to succeed, to be the best, to win. This built-in pressure to do better than others has produced outstanding results in inventiveness, material well-being, unusual wealth for some, and a nation that leads the world economically and politically. This same pressure has produced unintended and undesirable side effects, such as scamming—unethical schemes to con the unwary, the collapse of major economic institutions, and the disgrace of public figures.

It is true, our obsession with winning does produce winners, fair or foul, and the system usually rewards the one that comes out on top.

Just a few days prior to the outbreak of the Iraqi war, a national politician was speaking to a group of business executives about the impending

Competitive sports provide a clear example of the horrendous problem of containing the pressures of self-interest within appropriate bounds. In football, for example, the rules of acceptable and unacceptable behavior are well known to all participants. Each participant makes an individual, overt, prior commitment to abide by the rules. The field of play is small (300 feet by 160 feet), and the actions to monitor are few—at least when compared to the real-world geography of business and the many kinds of business an individual or organization can undertake. The complete rules of football can be condensed into one handy volume, albeit a thick one. But the laws and regulations of American business—federal, state, and local laws, and judicial precedents and also internal company policy guidelines, handbooks, memos, and unwritten codes or international and common laws—are strewn throughout massive, multivolume sets in thousands of national, state, county, and local archives.

To enforce the rules in football, seven referees are assigned to watch twenty-two players—a ratio of roughly one to three. These officials literally watch over the shoulders of the participants to keep behavior within the established bounds. Yet, even with all the enforcers, clear rules, small playing field, simple activities, and the ostensibly intrinsic pride of every participant to "play by the rules," the pressure of self-interest is still so intense that frequent gross violations of both ethical and legal behavior occur (holding, unnecessary roughness, interference, fakes, reverses, intimidation, etc.).

If abuses of self-interest cannot be controlled within the closely monitored competitive area of a football field, imagine what happens in the business world where the rules are not so clear, not always agreed upon by participants, and not monitored except by a few very remote referees.

CREATIVE MARKETING

People under such pressure and/or incentives can become very creative. A business professor in a management seminar once shared another example of the pressure to overstep ethical lines. He told attendees how, during a sabbatical leave from the university, he had discovered a company in Chicago that hired select college educators for six- to twelve-month internships. The company provided a hands-on business experience to the professors, who, in turn, could then give their students a more real-world understanding of how business works in the American economic system. Hopefully, they would also recommend a good student or two to work there. The speaker had applied and was accepted by the nationally known, medium-sized manufacturing company.

Near the end of his nine-month internship, the professor, along with another teacher from another company, was invited on a major Chicago radio show for an interview to discuss the teacher

(continued on next page)

war. One businesswoman asked the speaker, "With all the protest about this war, how will we deal with all the criticism even after we have won? Won't that dilute the victory?"

The successful politician told about running for his first national political office. He said, "I was running against a popular incumbent. On one occasion during the campaign, all the bankers and others of influence were hanging around the incumbent and I was being ignored because they thought he would win. Well, after the election when I won, everyone immediately dropped the incumbent and flocked around me. Winning has that influence on people. After we win the war, the protestors will go silent and most nations will come over to our side."

In our society it seems that with some few exceptions, the winner takes all. In sports, the gold medalist receives the recognition, the glory, the endorsements, the entry in the record books. Those placing a few seconds out of the medals are for the most part forgotten and ignored. As Vince Lombardi, an athletic coach very highly admired by business executives, put it, "Winning is not the most important thing, it is the only thing."

Tim Howells, former general manager of the Utah Jazz, may have best summed up the culture of winning when he said, "All we reward is winning. We don't reward people who have high values, integrity, or character."[7] The intensity of this widely held attitude can motivate people to indulge in questionable behavior to "grab the brass ring" or gold medal.

A few years ago, I was asked to be on a panel discussing ethics at a prominent regional university. Another member of the panel was Mr. Levine, one of the main players in the 1980s' Wall Street scandal of insider trading and other "improprieties." During the luncheon, we had an opportunity for an informal chat. Taking advantage of the moment, I asked, "Mr. Levine, you're a very rational, intelligent person, how did you get involved in this huge scandal?"

"In that high-powered, high-pressured environment," he said, "winning is the name of the game. The score is kept by how many deals you can make. In that wild, intense, pressured environment where winning has such very high rewards, there is neither time nor inclination to think about the subtleties of ethics."

Such pressures are found in much of the highly competitive business world. When a CEO has announced to Wall Street that her company projects a 19 percent growth rate for the coming year, the pressure gauge is set. As the year unfolds, everyone on the team knows the importance of meeting that result. As periodic progress checks are made, team members become fully aware of the punishments that lie in wait if the 19 percent goal is not met: The stock price drops, creating disgruntled shareholders, and lending institutions make it more expensive to raise needed capital. A great number of retirement fund values will be diminished when the value of the company's shares in their portfolios shrink. And a decline in stock value could threaten jobs in this company as well as cause the loss of expected bonuses. The pressure is high because there is a lot at stake.

internship program. The people at the radio station explained that the show was to be a discussion about a unique community interest education program, and was not to be advertising for a specific company.

However, in a preparation meeting at the company prior to going to the studio, the public relations director had told the interning professor, "Although this is supposed to be a community interest program, it provides us with an unusual opportunity to support the company's marketing effort. So for every mention of the company during the interview, we will give you $50. It will surely be worth that much to us in advertising."

The professor explained to the seminar attendees, "I came away from the experience with a tidy bonus. I also learned that, with the right motivation, marketing people can be made very creative. With that motivation, I surprised myself with how many ways I could bring the company's name into the conversation."

■   **AMPLE WIGGLE ROOM WITHIN RULE**

Area B affords ample opportunity for creativity while still allowing you to stay within the legal lines. Three examples will demonstrate what I mean.

First, the experience of the professor at the Chicago radio station shows what creative public relations people can do to promote the company's specific interest, and all are rewarded for doing so. (See "Creative Marketing" on this and previous page.)

The wishes and guidelines of the radio station were well understood, but pressure to promote the company's interests pressed the public relations director to find a way to step over the intended line and operate in Area B. No one did anything illegal, but it seems evident that both the director and the professor deliberately breached the ethical understanding regarding the rules of the interview and operated in Area B. And in so doing, their self-interests were, indeed, well served.

Second, creative people in charge of distribution have been known to stuff the distribution channels with inventory or label inventory as "sold" to make sales and inventory look better than it really is and possibly show that 19 percent growth rate.

Third, a creative accountant can find opportunities in Area B to make contributions to a company's image. Even with the Generally Accepted Accounting Principles there can be considerable wiggle room. A few years ago when professional baseball players went on strike over contract negotiations, there was a considerable number of public accusations. The players claimed the owners were making plenty enough profits to pay higher wages. The owners claimed the opposite, that there were just not enough profits to cover such large wage increases as the players demanded.

I remember hearing a press conference held by one of the owners. A reporter asked, "Are you making ample profits as the players claim or are you losing money?" The owner replied with a surprisingly frank response when he said, "When making my financial statements I can show my team lost $1 million or show that we made $2 million, and stay within GAAP. The players use one set of figures and we owners are entitled to use ours. That's how come you get these two claims."

Where there is such flexibility, it seems only natural for a business to show the picture that best fits its needs. Normally in annual financial reports, a CEO will want to paint the best picture possible of the company's performance, show the positive aspects of the company's performance in the most prominent way possible, and minimize or even hide its negative aspects as much as possible.

Embellishing financial statements to one degree or another is quite common practice. So common, in fact, that back in October of 1998, *Business Week* magazine sounded an alarm with "Forget about fraud for now. Regulators and investors are starting to focus on a far broader problem: companies bolstering their performance by using every legal accounting game in the book. They appear to be exploiting opportunities to jazz up their earnings like never before—all without stepping outside the loose confines of generally accepted accounting principles (GAAP)."[8]

This constant pressure of self-interest to overstep ethical and legal bound-
aries heightens for fear of losing one's competitive position when unscrupulous
practices on the part of one's competitor go unpunished by the business community. In industries, markets, or geographic areas where most competitors operate in
Area B, up against the legal line, it is extremely difficult for companies to operate
well within Area A and also stay in business. This problem is compounded because
the legal line often lacks a point of clear demarcation as to where illegality begins.
The ethical line is even less clearly defined—and thus more vulnerable to being
overstepped.

American companies that have operations in countries where bribes are the
norm, can have added pressure. In these countries it is often difficult for companies to get their share of the business without also operating in Areas B or C by giving
bribes. Some corporations will go so far as to hire top attorneys to find "loopholes"
in the law that will allow them to do many things their "less informed" competitors
may consider illegal. And when the law is unclear, "good attorneys," who have the
mission to help their companies obtain all the law will allow, can often assess the
risk of the behavior; what the chances are that the company would be found out,
what the combined damages and penalties could be; whether or not the action
could be successfully defended in court; whether
chief executives could be shielded from the burden
of responsibility; and so forth.

All these procedures demonstrate the constant, often intense, pressure to overstep not only
the ethical lines but also the legal lines.

So, when competition is intensifying, most of
the decisive play in Area A is up against the ethical
line where, from time to time, players step over
into Area B. When competition is very intense and
Area B—all the law will allow—is the primary playing field, we see the same results. As most of the
major action is up against the legal line, from time
to time the players will spill over into Area C—illegal
activities.

> One day a few years ago, I was ushered into the
> apartment of one of America's highly successful
> modern-day entrepreneurs. We had been personal
> friends for some time. He was on the phone and
> motioned for me to sit on the couch. Later he told
> me the phone call was a discussion with a banker
> about a $4 million loan for a manufacturing oper-
> ation in Japan. Of course I could only hear the en-
> trepreneur's side of the conversation. When my
> friend put forth an idea, apparently the banker
> had said, "That would be against the law." I heard
> my entrepreneur friend say, "There is no law that
> there isn't some way to get around it."

How does this happen to "honest" people? When pressures become intense, rationalization often sets in, either justifying that unethical actions are for a higher good or reasoning that the actions really aren't unethical after all because everyone is doing them, or they only hurt a few people, or the actions help people, or whatever. Selective perception, as discussed in Chapter One, greatly facilitates this rationalization and gives one a sense of being honest. I am not trying to imply that all managers overstep ethical or legal lines all the time, but the pressures to do so are constantly present to a greater or lesser degree.

■ THE NEED FOR COUNTERVAILING PRESSURE

Slogans such as "don't knock success," and "results sanctify the means," are examples of how our culture discourages serious questioning of means. Those who win or achieve the 19 percent growth are seldom checked up on or probed to detect whether they did anything unethical or illegal to reach it. More often they are cited as models for others to demonstrate that it can be done. But giving this behavior recognition reinforces it. It also announces to others that the questionable means that were used to gain the 19 percent are acceptable behavior in this company.

Oh, some executives may ask in passing, "Were you honest in achieving the 19 percent?" But when the answer is yes, the matter is dropped, and most often, the question is never raised. CEOs just assume without asking that everyone in their company in honest.

The fact is, if the superior should ask too frequently or probe deeply enough to expose unethical behavior, it would likely dampen the competitive spirit. Always harping on or stressing the subtleties of ethical behavior—enough to counter the pressures to step over the line—will seriously distract the focus and energy necessary to attain the results, make the goal, win.

This creates a difficult dilemma for any executive who is serious about establishing and maintaining an institution of integrity. One could consider reducing the pressure and thus lessen the temptation to step over the ethical or the legal line. But that would raise the risk of performing short of the goal.

SIX WAYS TO COUNTERACT PRESSURE

With such constant pressure to break through the structures and barriers that uphold, support, and reward ethical and legal behavior, some very strong counter-forces must be applied to reinforce them and keep them in place. Without significant pressure from the other side, these safeguards can collapse very easily, leaving little or no protection. In competitive business, what forces exist to counter the pressures to overstep the lines? Are they adequate to support and reward ethical behavior? What should we do to reward ethical behavior, strengthen ethical and legal lines, and reduce the frequency of their breach?

- **Recognize that people and companies face constant pressure to overstep ethical and legal lines in a competitive environment**. Moral decisions are not made in a protective vacuum. Although the intensity of that pressure may vary, its force is like a prevailing wind constantly blowing in the same direction and distorting ethical standards, just as persistent winds can distort the growth of trees.

  In all problem solving, recognizing and understanding the problem and its cause are an important first step to solving it. But until we can agree upon a cause, little appropriate action will happen. On the other hand, the mere awareness of the nature of self-interest pressures can provide the motivation and insight that lead to solutions.

- **Eliminate the source or reduce the intensity of competitive pressure whenever possible.** As one executive said, "If there is plenty of cash in the bank and profits are rising, it's not hard to be ethical." When profits are up, when the company faces no crisis in meeting payroll, when there is no criticism from shareholders about company performance, when no one is threatening a hostile takeover—in short, when things are going well, pressures to step over the lines are, though not absent, reduced. True, managers do not always have control over these sources of pressure, but managers can at least recognize the need for greater attentiveness to the ethical and legal lines—the need for strong counterforces.

- **Establish very clear and high personal standards for ethical behavior.** This requires two key elements: a) that businesspeople clearly determine and delineate for themselves what is ethical and what is unethical, and b) that they make a strong personal commitment to abide by ethical standards even in the face of danger. That is, they must be willing to endure any negative repercussions that may result from maintaining high ethical standards: poor results, diminished competitiveness, embarrassment, etc. Within the organization, top management must be willing to give positive reinforcement to those who abide by proper principles, even in the face of disappointing results.

- **Build a system of rewards within the organization that supports ethical and legal behavior and punishes unethical behavior.** Such a system would implement performance criteria to not only determine that desired results were attained but also to find out how well proper ethical procedures were followed or enforced. Too often in business, ethical issues are only discussed when the actions are so outrageous that the press or some outside group is likely to raise the issue and expose the wrongdoing.

- **Deliberately establish long-range strategies to ensure that ethical standards will eventually become automatic to the corporate culture.** They will become self-sustaining because the workers believe in and adhere to the standards both personally and professionally. Any corporation that has survived for any length of time has an ethical aspect to its culture. Companies would be wise to begin by carefully evaluating their culture—not in a witch hunt to root out past offenders (who may have been going along with the company's tolerance for unethical behavior), but in a focused effort to establish new working principles and procedures based on ethical practices. This means creating and allowing lots of discussion.

- **Employ someone responsible for riding herd on ethical and legal issues, either as a member of the board, as an internal consultant, or advisor.** Many organizations already have attorneys, accountants, human resources staff, and other "compliance officers," to help keep executives out of legal trouble. Ethical watchdogs, however, would need different qualifications and relationships.

Following these six steps will go a long way in establishing strong counter-forces to those pressures that produce undesirable behavior, and in creating a company with integrity.

After graduating from college, Stanley Mudrak spent five years with a reputable public accounting firm. His good work with the firm led to the break he hoped for: an excellent position in the Jason Manufacturing Company. During the first few months with his new company, Stanley watched the sales and profits decline rather drastically. He was confident, however, that the decline was only temporary and that in another month or two the market would adjust, the marketing campaign would run its course, and the company's sales and profits would be better than ever.

During this time, the company president called Stanley to his office. Evidently disturbed, the president told Stanley that the board of directors had just informed him of an unscheduled meeting for the following day. In the meeting, the president was to present the company's financial statements as of the end of the business day. The president knew that he was not the cause of the company's recent poor performance, but he feared that the board of directors would blame him, or at least hold him partially accountable for the slow turnaround. Like Stanley, he was confident that the firm's condition was temporary and would soon improve, but he felt that he might not convince the board on this point either. Accordingly, he requested that Stanley fix up the profit-and-loss statements to show a much smaller dip than had actually occurred. After all, he argued, better times were definitely coming and no one would be hurt if the statistics were altered.

Stanley knew the president to be a hard-driving but competent man, and he feared that the president would probably be hurt if the statistics were not altered.

QUESTIONS

1. If you were in Stanley Mudrak's position, what would you do and why?

2. What are the implications of questioning a leader's directions, knowing that most leaders prize unquestioning followership and loyalty?

3. If Stanley refuses to go along with the president, how will it impact his career?

4. What pressure, if any, is the president under?

5. In which area is the president asking Stanley to act?

**BE ALERT TO
INCREMENTAL
MORALITY**

CHAPTER FIVE

Incremental Morality

HERE IS ARTHUR ANDERSEN, one of America's premier international companies, not only in professional competence but also in its example of integrity. A few
months later it is completely destroyed by the exposure of its unethical behavior.
The tendency, in hindsight, is to say the company was run by corrupt people, as
though the night before it had been co-opted by the Mafia. A more useful question
would be, how could such good people engage in such outrageous behavior?

There *are* a few people in this world who start out with a deliberate scam in
mind, but they are the few. Most often, damning conduct begins with good people
pursuing noble ends, with noble means in mind in respectable institutions like
Arthur Andersen, Merrill Lynch, EDS, and HealthSouth. Something very gradual,
subtle, and insidious creeps into the organization to slowly infect the organizational body and incrementally eat away the healthy moral fiber.

Seldom does one see an executive jump from choirboy to crook in one leap.

■ THE FROG PRINCIPLE

Nearly everyone has heard a version of this or a similar story. I call the series
of justifications the "frog principle," and in one way or another, it makes criminals
of many.

Apparently (I've never tried it), if you drop a frog in a pan of hot water, the
shock causes it to jump out immediately to save its life. But if you place the frog in

John was just seventeen when he enlisted in the U.S. Marine Corps a year before World War II ended. Raised in a rural western farming town of about 500 people, he had never traveled more than 200 miles from his place of birth. Shortly after he turned nineteen, he was promoted to corporal and assigned to be the Marine Corps dispatcher for the motor pool on Treasure Island in San Francisco Bay—which proved to be an interesting eye-opener to the ways of the world.

Almost overnight, this unknown and insignificant enlisted man became someone of notice to many commissioned and non-commissioned officers. Many of these people began to approach him offering favors. For instance, the chief cook offered John a standing invitation to move to the head of the mess line at any meal and promised him fresh donuts and milk after hours. The manager at the theater made it easy for John to find a good seat, even if he arrived late, without having to stand in line. Duty officers suggested that he could have late night liberty whenever he desired without any hassle. The quartermaster even invited him to take advantage of "midnight requisitions"—extras of higher quality—of clothing and equipment beyond what normal standards permitted.

The attention and "thoughtfulness" of these people impressed John, and he felt fortunate that so many persons of influence wanted to be his "friends." Some of them even began to point out to him what a nice guy

a pan of cool water and gradually turn up the heat, it will stay in the pan until it is cooked. Frogs are cold-blooded, meaning their body temperature is consistent with their environment. So, it doesn't ever realize what is happening—it simply adapts and adjusts as the temperature rises—until it's too late. No alarm goes off to say it is time to jump.

Moral decay in individual lives and institutions most often follows this same pattern. Sometimes it's a kid at the cash register, but other times it's a bookkeeper, cash manager, professional accountant, or financial officer. Sometimes it's even a CEO who uses corporate perquisites for personal use, such as traveling in company jets to vacation destinations. In the beginning, only a small adjustment is made to meet a competitive situation or preclude some serious embarrassment. Then an-he was and how they knew they always could count on him. Soon he began to receive many friendly requests from these generous new friends for rides to San Francisco or Oakland. No problem, he thought. He simply could ask the driver of the vehicle going that way to take the person along. All he had to do was coordinate the time and instruct the driver.

From time to time, John might instruct a driver to travel a few blocks or maybe a mile out of the assigned way to accommodate the needs of a "special passenger." After all, it would only be fair since many of these "special passengers" had gone out of their way to accommodate his needs on occasion.

As time went on, these special friends began to be more and more generous. On the other hand, they also began to make more and more requests for transportation that was farther and farther away from couriers' routes. But it was quite easy to accommodate them since no one ever checked up, and he could always find ample ways to cover for the extra miles and time.

Looking back as a mature man, John was glad that he had been discharged before things got out of hand. He hadn't noticed anything wrong at the time, but as he reflected on his time at Treasure Island, he remembered that he had become confident and bold with his power to make decisions without supervision, sometimes stepping over the ethical line and often coming perilously close to stepping over the legal line. It would only have been a matter of time.

other and another. Recognizing how unethical behavior begins (almost imperceptibly) and then grows (in almost unseen increments) is necessary if one is going to implement policies to curb immoral behavior.

Most people face this same dilemma in business settings. Many times, young workers are hired into organizations, bringing their lofty ideas about being totally honest with them. If a manager or mentor tells them to "work around the truth" or "tell them only what they need to know," the idea is abhorrent to them, and they often refuse. But, when it becomes a matter of losing a job or making a good impression, the pressure builds and small rationalizations begin: "I just won't say anything as long as they don't *ask*," or "It's not actually lying since what I've said is *technically correct*," or "I wouldn't want to jeopardize our negotiating position."

The frog principle seems to be at play in every walk of life. I can still remember when basketball was a "non-contact" sport. I would get called for a foul for simply resting my hand on the back of an opposing player I was guarding so I could keep track of his movement while I watched the ball. Since then, the sport has allowed players to escalate such practices that now include pushing, shoving, and other aggressive moves that maintain an advantage, especially when going after the ball. Of course, these would not be called pushing and shoving anymore. Now, it's "blocking out," "setting the screen," "posting up," "incidental contact," and even "no harm, no foul." If the present course continues, basketball players will have to start wearing protective gear like that of hockey or football players.

Then, when the tactics work as planned, the employees notice that such a strategy gets results. Any guilt they might feel for violating their personal standards of integrity is efficiently swept away by the feeling of success.

When the situation comes up again, these young employees find it more difficult to hold to their personal standard. After all, "it's just a little exaggeration or understatement," they reason. Or, if they resist this time, the manager might say, "What's wrong now? You did it before."

Those who have lost their awareness of such subtle dilemmas soon begin to *believe* that "it's not actually lying." Like the proverbial frog, they soon find themselves over their heads in hot water, usually without realizing it.

The pressure for results can make it hard to see any red flags or stop signs, if there are any, that might say "not one step further." Instead, each successive degree seems like only one little step from the last one—"What's the harm in this much more?"

For example, many politicians go to Washington or state capitals on the strength of their idealism and the votes of their constituents. Often they promise to avoid becoming victims of powerful lobbyists, but most of them soon change. As the pressure to get reelected builds, they soon see the need to resort to "common practice." They accept, or even begin to elicit, large campaign contributions from the lobbies so they can keep their campaigns alive.

■ THE SLIPPERY SLOPE

The path seems so obvious and clear to observers who compare the before and after, but the incline is so slight, and the descending steps so small, that no alarm goes off or demands attention until the jailhouse doors clang and we wonder, "What happened? When did I step over the line?"

One of the bright young men involved in the Watergate affair commented on the subtlety and blinding nature of this seduction when, after all things were exposed, he said, "In the heat of the battle, we not only thought we were doing the right thing, but the righteous thing."

Most people agree that honesty is right and safe legal territory, and fraud is very unsafe and quite wrong. But with so many steps and shades of unethical behavior in between the two extremes, and so many of them used in a business setting, no one seems to be willing or able to identify where the ethical or legal lines are that would warn someone if he or she were about to overstep the bounds. Placing some of them on a continuum, we have:

> Honesty
> > Withholding information
> > > "Puffery" and public relations
> > > > "Little white" lies
> > > > > Leading to believe
> > > > > > Exaggeration and understatement
> > > > > > > Evading or stretching the truth
> > > > > > > > Saying things that are not so
> > > > > > > > > Fraud

Using these notches along the honesty-to-fraud continuum as benchmarks, where would you categorize your accounting reports, financial statements, explanations for declining stock prices, sales pitches, press releases, stories to associates at the water cooler or friends at the local hangout, comments about people's job performance, observations about others' lifestyle choices or personal habits, your résumé or job applications, your taxes?

A report by John Curran of the Associated Press gives one a feel for the subtlety of this slippery slope in the competitive marketplace.

> The half-gallon ice cream container—the sweet standard of grocery store freezers for decades—is starting to shrink.
>
> While manufacturers over the years reduced the package size of everything from candy bars to dish detergent, the traditional ice cream "brick" remained what it was—the half-gallon.
>
> Now, pinched by rising ingredient costs and afraid to raise prices already at about $5 for many brands, at least two ice-cream makers have started silently phasing out the half-gallon with a 1.75 quart carton, a half-pint smaller.
>
> Dreyer's, which is based in Oakland, California, and sells Dreyer's and

Edy's brands, began introducing the smaller package in March. The new and old cartons can be found side-by-side during the transition, identical in shape and design—and price. But one has two quarts, the other $1^3/4$.

"We have over 100 flavors and many of them—because people are preferring indulgent, chunky flavors—cost more to produce than regular flavors like vanilla," said Dreyer's spokesman Dori Bailey. "We'd like to keep the cost at a price that's more affordable for folks."

Some customers are noticing the change and don't appreciate it. "Everyone's doing it," complained Dorothy McGrath, 73, as she shopped the ice-cream aisle at a Super Fresh supermarket in Egg Harbor Township, N.J. "The same thing happened with laundry detergent. The brands I used to buy in 100-ounce bottles are now 80-ounces, only the price is the same. They're cheating the public, because they don't advertise it."[1]

Is Dorothy right, are the companies "cheating" the public? Should a company of integrity be expected to "advertise" the change? Is this one of those small, subtle steps down the slippery slope? Undoubtedly, in discussing this ice cream incident, there will be significant disagreement. While some will contend this is deception, others will just as sincerely argue, "Certainly not. One and three-fourths quarts is clearly marked on the container."

An institution that wants to identify itself with integrity must discuss and rediscuss the problem of incremental morality with specific examples like the ice-cream carton one. If in your company this practice is acceptable, say so and explain why. Then cite a nearby example that is not acceptable and say why not, so each employee knows where the line is and has a red flag to guide them. Just repeating a vague platitude, "Don't get caught by creeping morality," is not enough.

■   **POWER SEDUCES**

The seduction of power and success abets the Frog Principle. One of my early career experiences demonstrates how subtly self-interest and one's business environment can first blind, then trap you—inch by inch, step by step.

Shortly after I entered college, I gained part-time employment as an accountant with the State Road Commission. This paralleled very nicely with my major field of study—accounting. I worked half-days during school times and full-time during the summer. I was assigned to a desk and work area in the district office staffed by a small cadre of engineers and office workers.

The state was divided into six districts. Our district was responsible for maintaining the highways and roads in the northern part of the state, work that included repairing signs and guardrails, clearing rocks from the roads and drains, patching and resurfacing roads, and removing snow. The work was carried out by groups of workers assigned to various "shops" placed in strategic locations around the district. The employee roster was made up of sixty to a hundred outdoor laborers and equipment operators.

One summer, the state governor began to take a personal interest in the U.S. savings bond payroll-deduction plan. He had discovered that the number of state employees who had signed up for the plan was low, and he determined to change it. His staff prepared a special packet of instructions for each district, which included a letter above the governor's signature along with sign-up forms and brochures that gave reasons why everyone should participate.

The governor's letter asked that each district designate someone to be responsible for the bond drive. The district superintendent asked me to be in charge. I suggested that because I was a junior employee and only temporary, I would not be a wise choice, but he insisted. After all, we were neighbors, and he said he would help me. One phrase in the letter struck me as odd, but it later became very useful: "When the drive is completed, please send directly to me a list of names of those who did not sign up for the U.S. savings bond payroll-deduction plan."

The district office where I worked sent a packet similar to the governor's to each employee in the district that included all the information from the governor's office plus a letter from the district superintendent indicating that I had been placed in charge of the drive. But the superintendent was skeptical that that alone would interest these hard-bitten, outdoor workers in the payroll-deduction scheme, so to increase our chances of signing up more people, he wrote in his letter that I would be paying each of them a personal visit.

At first I was reluctant to take the assignment because I felt it was hypocritical to ask people to sign up for the plan when I didn't intend to sign up. I needed to save all the money I could for my school expenses. Still, I couldn't turn down the superintendent; he had been the one who got me the job in the first place, and who had been sort of a personal mentor to me. I hoped that by just passing out the information I could get by.

But as we discussed that method, he convinced me that these maintenance men were a skeptical lot and would just as soon not be bothered by handouts or mail. We designed a campaign to overcome their resistance. The superintendent had a no-nonsense leadership style, and everyone knew that he was a political appointee. In addition, the people who worked for him knew that he controlled their jobs largely at his pleasure. In our campaign, we were to use this information to our advantage: A critical part of our strategy was that I would personally accompany the superintendent in his truck to each work site. While he took care of his regular business, I would speak to each employee personally. We figured that if the workers saw me get out of the truck with the superintendent, they would think twice before turning down the invitation to sign up. We supposed that if they gave me a hard time, they would think I would report the conversation to the superintendent as we drove off.

When I approached the first workers and stated my mission, I could sense a grudging deference toward me. One man brought me up short when he challenged, "Yeah? How much have you signed up for?" I was on the spot. In the crisis of the moment, I said, "I'm signing up for the recommended amount." He assumed that I had signed up, which I hadn't. I did nothing to correct his conclusion, for I didn't want to reduce my already-limited authority to influence. So, the way he understood my comment made me untruthful. After the fact, I corrected the situation by returning to the truck and filling out a payroll deduction slip for myself, but now I was trapped. I had been forced, by not wanting to lose face, to do two things I did not want to do: 1) be deceitful, and 2) sign up for the payroll deduction plan. From then on, I determined I would speak honestly about my own position.

Although the positive arguments for U.S. savings bonds in the brochure didn't do much to overcome the workers' evident reluctance, the subtlety of me stepping out of the superintendent's truck seemed to help a lot. I heard casual comments like, "You must be the boss's drinking buddy," or "How come you're in so good with the boss?" If that didn't carry the day, I would casually mention the governor's statement of wanting a list. In my mind, it wasn't a threat. My rationale was that it wouldn't be right to go behind their backs and send in their names without letting them know up front. Usually just a comment about the governor's statement was enough.

Things had gone so well that near the end of the drive, all but three men had signed up for the plan. When I reported the results to the superintendent and other key people in the office, the 100 percent fever began to rise. "Wouldn't it be great to get 100 percent? No other district is going to do it. We would be the only ones." We huddled and conspired—excuse me, I mean "strategized." We decided that the superintendent would call the three men and appeal to their loyalty and team spirit. "Look, we are so close to 100 percent, please don't let the team down." None of them budged.

More strategizing. People in the office reiterated what a shame it would be if we didn't get 100 percent—we were so close. We just couldn't stop now. What a feather in our cap we would have if we could get those last three. Everyone in the Road Commission would recognize what we had done. Surely it would not go unnoticed in the governor's office either, because there would be few, if any, other 100 percent departments. We decided that I should go back to visit with the men one more time.

By this time, I understood that my reputation around the office had a chance for major upgrading. If I could pull this off, I reasoned, I would be seen as some-one who "knows how to get things done," even though I was still quite young. My name would be on the final report that would go to the governor: "Governor, we are happy to report that we have 100 percent subscription in our department"—and then my signature.

My personal energy, commitment, and creativity were now fully combined. Along with some suggestions from the people at the district office, I set out on my appointed mission determined to reach the new goal. With the first man I pleaded, cajoled, and mildly threatened that others in the district might regard him unfa-vorably for letting the team down, and I again reminded him of the governor's statement. After my reminder, he paused a minute as he tried to assess the possible implications, and then he shook his head no.

In my mind, I now believed that this would be good for the district and also very good for him. After all, he was not a saver and this would be an important start for him. With all this moral justification and reasoning on my side, in desperation I pulled out of my folder a letter that I would be sending the governor that showed his name among the three lonely names standing out on the page surrounded by a sea of white. As I pulled it out I thought to myself, "I do not want to put undue pressure on him." My only desire was to give him all the information possible so that he could make an informed decision. After all, I was only trying to look out for *his* interests.

He took the letter from my hand and studied it for some time. Finally, he set the letter down, and in a very resigned voice said, "All right, what's the minimum amount?" He then filled out the sign-up slip. Then, conspicuously and with a broad smile, I took a pen from my pocket, and with a larger-than-necessary motion, crossed off his name. He didn't seem all that happy, but he did seem somewhat relieved.

With the second man, I repeated the same sales performance, except now the governor's letter showed only the two names with another name crossed out. Reluctantly, he signed up for the minimum. Then he asked, "How long do I have to wait before I can cancel this deduction?" I was now beaming. Only one more to go!

The last man twinged my conscience a little because he had a large family, and it was already hard for him to make ends meet. But, for a true salesman like me caught up in the 100 percent fever, I rationalized that with his big family, it was even more important for him to save. In fact, it was the *best* thing for him, even if he didn't realize it. When I showed him the letter with only his name on it, he paused for a moment, but he still balked. Then, still aching for that 100 percent goal, I remembered the previous man's question and proposed, "Look, why don't you just sign up for the minimum, and then after you get your first check with the deduction, you can call up the office and cancel the deduction? This will save us from sending your name to the governor [pause] . . . and you won't be an embarrassment to the team by single-handedly keeping them from reaching 100 percent [pause] . . . and you'll be out practically no money at all [pause] . . ." I pushed the sign-up slip toward him already filled out, wanting only a signature.

He stared at it for a moment. Then he said, "Oh, what the hell." He took my pen, scribbled his name on the slip, pushed the pen and paper back, stood up, and left. Again, I felt a little twinge of something—but only for a moment until I could sense my success.

"Yeah! One hundred percent!"

The report went in. Recognition came back, even more than we had expected. The other districts in the state inquired, "How did you do it?" We received a personal letter from the governor. The superintendent was overjoyed. And I had learned how to sell successfully.

But did I do it ethically? At the time, I was confident that I had. It was just good ol'-fashioned American can-do know-how right?

Since then, I have had many second thoughts about that experience. No one asked a single question about the propriety or ethics of my methods. Most people were simply awed by the skill and competence of a good young man. It was mostly a matter of laud and fame for me. Well, some of the employees may have felt that they had been unduly influenced. Maybe they were the victims of some subtle trickery, even subterfuge. I have often wondered how the last three men had interpreted the experience. I wonder if they might even have a legitimate claim that they had been blackmailed.

In hindsight, it now seems obvious to me that the not-so-subtle pressure of the 100 percent fever and the seduction of success pushed me over an ethical line and maybe even the legal line. The most embarrassing aspect about that experience is that, at the time, in the heat of the battle, I barely saw any of those questionable things, and only for a brief moment. The reflections coming off the gold pot of success overwhelmed all those other little subtleties.

They also blinded me from noticing my own mixed motives. In this case, the prime self-interest motive was the recognition I would get for achieving the 100 percent goal. My public or stated motive was to save a worker the embarrassment that would come from sending his name to the governor. Very often in the creeping morality process, we develop noble rationalizations to self-justify each small step.

Back to the question at the beginning of this chapter: How could a noble company like Arthur Andersen get involved in such ignoble behavior that it would self-destruct? Of course, no one, single answer explains everything. However, the slippery slope of incremental morality would be one significant part of the catastrophe.

■   REVERSING THE SLIDE

Stopping the slide is difficult. It requires decisiveness, resoluteness, firmness, and strong resistance to the argument, "this next step is really very small."

Reversing the slide is much more difficult than stopping it. Once the practice is in place, it is easy to be swayed with the innocent, "Look it worked and no harm was done." Setting policies to move back up to a level of real integrity is a bit like repairing the leaky roof. When it's not raining, "why worry?" And, when it is raining, "you can't get up on the roof in a storm."

Although deliberate efforts to move back up the slope towards honesty may meet with initial resistance or discomfort—even competitive disadvantage and financial loss—over time these efforts can engender great respect and trust.

Maybe in the end, the bottom line is just how big a price you are willing to pay for integrity.

■ **WHAT TO DO ABOUT CREEPING ETHICS**

Any institution serious about integrity must take seriously the challenge of countering and controlling creeping ethics. Here are some suggestions for making a start:

■ **1. RECOGNIZE THE FROG PRINCIPLE.** People talk about and look for deceit, lies, fraud, and greed as though they are bright, gaudy banners for everyone to see, so why doesn't the Securities and Exchange Commission (SEC) go after them while they are happening instead of waiting until things fall apart? The reason is that the accumulation of little steps of wrongdoing are seldom obvious during the creeping destructive stage. Deliberately look for and focus on those small, marginal acts.

■ **2. DEVELOP A CULTURE THAT NOTICES SMALL MISSTEPS.** A memo will not do. A meeting will not do. There is no substitute for talk and re-talk followed by administrative action to get the message across that those small first missteps are warning signs in this organization.

■ **3. ESTABLISH WHERE ON THE SLIPPERY SLOPE YOU WILL PLANT A RED FLAG.** Because there is often such a fine line between approved behavior and wrong behavior, this requires a concerted effort. It will be necessary to discuss several actual incidents in your company that are very near the line, but on the right side, and some that are very near the line, but are on the wrong side. Discussing situations that are clear and

> When the cumulative little misdeeds begin to unravel, the end looms large and evil. It takes the careful eye of a sleuth to detect those first marginal violations of integrity:
>
> When the Securities & Exchange Commission on March 19 [2003] charged HealthSouth Corp. with faking $1.4 billion in profits since 1999, the question was obvious: Where were the auditors? In a post–Arthur Andersen world, it is surprising that Ernst & Young, the largest audit firm in the country, could have missed one this big. Even Richard P. Wessel, head of SEC's Atlantic office, seemed amazed. "It is shocking that you could have a misstatement of income and revenues of this extent just since 1999," he says. And it may be even worse: the SEC alleges that HealthSouth began inflating its numbers from its start in 1986.[2]

obviously on one side or the other will not clearly demark a line that will catch those small, first missteps. It's that small, marginal first step that starts the slide, which must be clearly identified.

■ **4. PLANT A RED FLAG.** Once the boundary is determined, "draw a line in the sand" by rewarding those who stay on the right side—even if it loses a sale. Penalize those who take even just a small step over it, so everyone knows where the line is and takes it seriously.

■ **5. MAINTAIN THE LINE OF DEMARCATION.** Unless a rigorous vigilance is maintained to keep the line visible—the line in the sand clear—competitive pressures will fill in the sand and make the line hard or impossible to see. Regularly raise penetrating questions regarding how goals and successes are being achieved. Remember, benign neglect is one of the best ways for incremental morality to get out of hand.

To be alert and probing for evidence of those small ethical violations without dampening the competitive spirit or the will to achieve established goals is a major challenge for anyone desiring the label, "An Institution of Integrity."

CASE: QUARTERLY REPORTS

Marc had spent a few years working for a small CPA firm before he switched to a private start-up construction company to work as the company's accounting manager.

"I was in charge of preparing financial statements for preparation of tax returns and submission to investors and lending institutions to acquire financing for the company. The information that you want to present to these two audiences is in direct conflict with each other. For tax purposes, you want the company to make as little money as possible, thereby reducing the amount of taxes that it pays. To acquire financing, you want the company to make as much money and look as good as possible to enhance the terms of your financing.

"This small company was able to acquire limited financing during its first year of business solely from the promise and guarantee of its owners. Midway through the second year, the banks wanted to see the progress that the company was making and decide whether to continue to extend credit to the company based on its year-to-date financial statements. As a matter of practice, the company did not recognize income until the property it had built actually changed ownership to the buyer or closed. Unfortunately, by the end of the second quarter, there had been very few closings. Only about 20 percent of the year's projected closings had taken place prior to the end of the second quarter.

"After I prepared the initial financial statements, I reviewed them with the company's owner and president. We knew that if we submitted these statements the way that they looked, our chances of the bank continuing to extend credit would be very low, if not impossible. As we examined the company's work, we discovered that there were several closings scheduled within the next few weeks. The president said that if we would recognize the sales from those closings prior to the end of the second quarter, it would make the financial statements look nearly twice as good as they did now.

"There was a great risk that if we did *not* get a continuation of credit from the bank, the company would likely suffer so badly that it would go out of business. This would adversely affect the lives of not only the company owners, but also the employees and all of the vendors and suppliers that the company provides work for. The company president instructed me to book these sales prior to the end of the quarter and redo the financial statements for the bank.

"I changed the books to recognize the sales for all the contracts we had that were scheduled to close in the next few weeks and delivered them to the bank. Subsequently, the company got a continuation of its credit and had a very successful year.

1. Was Marc a man of integrity? Was his boss?

2. Were you in Marc's position, would you have agreed to the president's request or would you have refused? What were his alternatives?

3. Even though the sales-booking process was far enough along they were "sure to close," and in fact they did, was booking the sales a few weeks early just a small step on the slope?

4. When does a sale actually take place? When the buyer commits to the purchase? Or only after all the paperwork is done?

5. Next time similar pressure arises will it be ok to book as sales all that will close in the next two months?

6. Where should the president plant the flag on this slippery slope? Two weeks? Four weeks? Six weeks? Or back at close only?

CHAPTER SIX

Moral Ethics vs. Gaming Ethics

*To hold up a standard of applying, in any literal sense to work-a-day life,
the teaching of the Judeo-Christian tradition [the Golden Rule] is to put an
impractical, if not impossible, burden upon management. It is tantamount to
no less than projecting the executive group into a situation of perpetual
sinfulness.* "[1]

Benjamin Selekman

FACING UP TO THE DIFFICULTY if not impossibility of applying lofty moral
ideals to the practical business world is a challenge of major proportions. Benjamin
Selekman, a former professor of Labor Relations at the Harvard Graduate School
of Business has stated the problem most succinctly.

Richard B. Haws, president of Multi-Products, Inc., was speaking with his
friend and lamenting how "the average young man today has no concept of how to
beat a competitor and how to squeeze money out of every dollar." Picking up his
office *Who's Who,* Haws showed his friend that he had attended college for three
years, worked as a salesman in a local business for another five, and then moved to
New York in 1929 to sell for the Lawton Machinery Company:

> We were living in a nice apartment and had all our money in the market when
> the crash came. I went to our landlord and asked him to let me break the
> lease, but he pointed out that he needed money more than ever now, and re-
> fused. I went home to think about it, and then returned and pleaded with
> him to let us move to one of his cheaper apartments. Finally, he agreed. He
> moved us the next day and that night brought up a new lease for me to sign.

I looked him in the eye and said, "Oh, no. When you moved us out of that first apartment, you broke the lease. We're moving out of here tomorrow." That's the sort of sharp thinking—in that case born out of financial necessity—that young men don't seem to use today. They certainly don't learn it in business schools.[2]

Is that just "sharp thinking" as Haws claims, or is this deceitful behavior? This question often evokes animated controversy. Some argue that Haws is playing by the rules: He broke no law; he just took advantage of the law. Others argue that he did not play by the rules because he deliberately deceived the landlord.

Who is right? That depends upon which set of rules you apply to the situation. One of the fundamental ethical problems in our society is that everyone carries around two different, distinct—and legitimate—sets of ethical standards. I don't mean a good one and a bad one, just two different, valid and morally defensible, commonly accepted standards. The argument arises not because there is a group of people with "bad" ethics and a group with "good" ethics, but when one party believes the "x" set of ethics is appropriate in a given situation, and the other party believes the "y" set of ethics is what should apply to the same circumstances. And because most people fail to recognize that everyone employs two distinct sets of rules in their daily lives, we never can deal with the problem effectively.

■ A DOUBLE STANDARD

At this point, you may feel like scolding me, "You may use two standards, but I certainly don't. I have one standard, which is my measure in every facet of my life." But let's test that declaration:

First, everyone I know has one standard that I call "personal ethics," or "religious ethics." Under this set of rules, most of us would generally agree that it's wrong to deliberately mislead or deceive another person, or to steal. We also would agree that it's wrong to identify another person's weakness and then deliberately design a scheme to take advantage of that weakness for personal gain. In other words, under this set of ethics we live the Golden Rule.

FOUR ELEMENTS OF ETHICS	PERSONAL ETHICS
1. Deliberately mislead	Wrong
2. Deliberately deceive	Wrong

3. Take advantage of another's weakness for personal gain	Wrong
4. Steal	Wrong

So why do we so often deliberately mislead others, or consciously deceive people and intentionally take advantage of their weaknesses for our own personal gain, and even steal—all the time thinking that we have done nothing against the Golden Rule?

"I would never do such a thing," you say.

"Oh yes you do, and you either do it or approve of it all the time," I insist.

"When would I ever deliberately do such a thing?" you ask.

I am glad you asked.

The last time you played a game of tennis, did you ever deliberately lead your opponent to believe that you were going to return the ball cross court, when all along you knew you were going to send it right down the alley? Or, when playing poker, did you ever try to lead the other players—through your facial expressions—to believe that you had a poor hand, when all along you held a Royal Flush? Or, in a game of chess, have you ever caused your opponent to change his or her mind because you grinned openly as the person considered moving a key piece to a new position, when all along you didn't have the faintest idea what you could do to stop your devastating losses? Have you ever watched a champion athlete such as a basketball player, football quarterback, or volleyball spiker who was unskilled in the art of deception—head fakes, double pumps, quick steps, hidden-ball tricks, intimidation, etc.? Have you ever cheered with joy when the opponent of your favorite team drops the ball or gets penalized so that your team wins the game?

"Ah," you say, "Those are games, and there are different rules for competitive games."

Very good. You are getting the picture.

In competitive games, the rules, or ethics, are different than in personal life. I call this second set of rules, "gaming ethics" or "sporting ethics." In gaming ethics, deliberately misleading and deceiving others is not only allowed, but it's an essential skill for winning. To take advantage of another's weakness is not only allowed, but is expected of good players. If, in a competitive game of tennis, you discover that your opponent has a weak backhand, it is ethical to drill the ball to that backhand as much as possible. In football, quarterbacks are expected to identify weaknesses in the defense and then intentionally throw or run the ball in that direction—all for their own gain. In baseball, stealing bases is a good strategy for base runners; in football and basketball, stealing the ball is one of the objects of defense. When playing chess, if your opponent inadvertently makes a poor move or choice, if you are playing seriously, you are expected to take advantage of the situation before the person recognizes the mistake. Under gaming ethics, we take advantage of all that the rules allow.

FOUR ELEMENTS OF ETHICS	PERSONAL ETHICS	GAMING ETHICS
1. Deliberately mislead	Wrong	Okay
2. Deliberately deceive	Wrong	Okay
3. Take advantage of another's weakness for personal gain	Wrong	Okay
4. Steal	Wrong	Okay

So we agree that there *are* two sets of ethical standards: "personal ethics," in which we never deliberately mislead or deceive other people or intentionally take advantage of their weaknesses for personal gain; and "gaming ethics," in which purposely misleading or deceiving other people, or stealing, is not only allowed, but encouraged, practiced, and perfected, and taking advantage of another's weakness for personal gain is the best way to play the game.

Most people try to govern their personal lives by personal ethics, and in competitive games they apply gaming ethics. I think that most people understand this behavioral switch, and few are upset by it.

"So what's the problem?" you ask.

In sports, it is quite clear that abiding by "gaming ethics"—misleading, deceiving, taking advantage and stealing—is quite appropriate. The problem is where else in life are gaming ethics accepted? How about war? It surely seems okay to mislead and deceive in this circumstance. War strategy *particularly* focuses on the enemy's weaknesses. Stealing or destroying the enemy's supplies is an obvious yes.

How about politics? In a campaign, it seems quite all right to point out all of the opponent's weaknesses and never mention a single strength, while doing just the opposite for one's self. Is this an attempt to mislead? Taking advantage of an opponent's embarrassing statement or controversial vote seems acceptable practice.

How about courtship? Is making a concerted effort to show one's very best side while keeping negative characteristics hidden not just part of the dating game? Is that conveying a true impression? Taking advantage of a girl's weakness for shiny cars doesn't seem unethical. In our society, it also seems quite acceptable to steal another person's girlfriend or boyfriend if you can.

Clearly, some aspects of gaming ethics are followed without hesitation in areas of life other than just sports.

■ THE $64,000 QUESTION

Now for the big question: Which set of rules should you live by in the competitive business world? Is business a competitive game ruled by gaming ethics, or an extension of our personal life that we ought to govern by the higher standard of personal ethics?

I first learned about the problem of two conflicting sets of ethical standards when I read an article by Albert Carr in the *Harvard Business Review*. Carr wrote, "If an executive allows himself to be torn between a decision based on business consideration [gaming ethics] and one based on his private ethical code [personal ethics], he exposes himself to a grave psychological strain."[3]

Both Carr and Selekman (page 70) suggest that business is a competitive game, where gaming ethics may be appropriate, even unavoidable. If a football quarterback tries to avoid all deception, he will win very few games. Executives who attempt to avoid all deception will have trouble building a successful business, and if they fail to take advantage of competitors' weaknesses in products, services, contacts, or information, they will lose business to their competitors who practice gaming ethics.

The best-selling author of a book about real estate was a guest on an early-morning national talk show, discussing his new book. The interviewer asked him, "What is the essence of your book?"

He responded, "The key is to find someone who has a great desire to sell, so you can get property for a very good price."

A panel member quickly reacted, "I believe it's ethically wrong to take advantage of someone else's economic misfortune."

The author's defense was simply, "Look, this is the best-selling book ever on real estate."

In his book, the author explains about searching for "don't wanters"—people who don't want their property. In the real-estate world, of course, the term is a euphemism for people who are desperate to sell. Exploiting another's economic desperation for our own personal gain may not be an ethical principle most of us would advocate as part of our personal code, but many people have little or no hesitation about acting this way in a business setting.

The panelist and the author are examples of the two different philosophies. The panelist advocated applying personal ethics to the situation: Even though it is legal and profitable to do what the author suggested, the recommendation violated the panelist's ethical code, which was that you do not exploit the desperation of another person to your own advantage. The author, on the other hand, saw gaming ethics as appropriate to the situation, much like a poker game: The key to success in the competitive world is to take advantage of all the law or rules will allow, and this is not wrong if all parties will argue gaming ethics is legitimate.

Negotiating is an area of particular challenge. When negotiating with labor unions, a potential merger partner, or a supplier, which set of ethics do you follow? If you are completely up-front with all your information and openly share exactly what you will or will not do, holding nothing back, there is no room to negotiate. Negotiation is a game of using information and other techniques to gain position or gain advantage. Don't give away too much too easily. Is not gaming ethics the understood guide for negotiations?

Take another look at Mr. Haws, the business executive quoted at the beginning of the chapter. Is he ethical or unethical? Clearly, if we hold the standard of personal ethics to the world of business, he behaved unethically: He deliberately deceived the landlord. But if we believe that business is a competitive game, then gaming ethics are appropriate and Mr. Haws has been as upright and ethical as any football quarterback.

When businesspeople fail to distinguish between the two sets of rules, confusion, frustration, and accusations abound—especially when one person thinks personal ethics are the best standard for the situation and another thinks gaming ethics are the way to go.

Looking at the practice of raising and marketing salmon produced in "farms" in contrast to wild salmon demonstrates the difficulty of identifying the rules when there is no rule book in print.

Food coloring is a product readily available on the market, so can it be concluded that coloring food is a commonly accepted ethical practice?

Coloring salmon "naturally" has some people so morally outraged that they have filed a lawsuit against three of America's largest and most respected grocery chains, Kroger Co., Safeway, and Albertsons. According to accuser Paul Kampmeier, "Pink sells salmon. To artificially color salmon without giving that information to consumers,

(continued on page 76)

(continued from page 75)

we believe that's unfair and deceptive, and it's against federal law."

According to the reporter, Linda Ashton, "The flesh of farmed salmon is naturally grayish, and the salmon are given special food to alter their hue to a more desirable shade."

The British Columbia Salmon Farmer's Association's Web site notes that "Wild salmon's brightly colored flesh is the result of cartenoid pigment the fish get from eating krill or small crustaceans. The same pigments are added to the diets of farmed fish."

Further, the report says, "Salmon farms allow consumers to get the fish fresh year-round at inexpensive prices."[4]

When fish get their coloring from the food they eat, is that "natural" coloring or "artificial" coloring? After all, these salmon are not being spray painted prior to display. Does integrity require the label to detail the diet of the animal marketed for food? Geography alone would cause animals of the same species to have variations in their diets. For instance, salmon caught in the fresh water of the River Naver in the north of Scotland display gray rather than pink flesh.

In the business world of competition where the "rule book" is incomplete, determining what is right and what is wrong can indeed be a challenge.

GAMING ETHICS AREN'T A FREE-FOR-ALL

But don't be misled into thinking that gaming ethics is an "anything goes" kind of a setting. The parameters are different than those of personal ethics, but the "do's and don'ts" *are* there. Sometimes rule books spell out the details or the law has decreed it will be thus, so there is enough specificity to give guidelines. Integrity, however, is the kind of behavior that is guided by what's "right and wrong" beyond the legal. In this non-legalized field is where persons of integrity distinguish themselves.

So how can you determine the proper behavior in fields where the law does not speak, where the informal or intangible "understood" moral values are expected to govern? Short of a decree from Mt. Sinai or Mt. Washington, how can your business know what is proper?

When it comes to the informal rules of "right and wrong," "common practice" does make a contribution. In most societies, when all or most people engage in a specific behavior, it is an indication of what is acceptable. When all or most people disapprove of a specific behavior, it is an indication of what is unacceptable. Combining these two is one way of identifying the right and wrong of any particular society, culture, or industry. Common practice then, can be a guideline to proper behavior.

But just a minute. Does that mean if everyone else is doing it, that makes it all right? The idea cannot be ignored.

According to Erin McClain[5], in WorldCom CFO Scott Sullivan's defense suit, he is going to show that "other telecom executives use similar accounting methods—including accounting short-term "line" expenses as long-term capital expenditures—meaning that for accounting purposes the cost could be spread over many years instead of charged in the year the expense occurred."

According to a former Justice Department prosecutor, Christopher Bebel, "The closer Sullivan gets to establishing that these practices were employed on a widespread basis, the more likely he is to secure a not-guilty verdict." [6]

Common practice does seem to be a quick guide to what is acceptable behavior. It may even be what establishes ethical standards in gaming ethics.

■ EVERYONE FEELS A NEED TO BE FAIR

"Just live the golden rule" is the solution to any ethical problem so frequently given by managers that it is worthy of closer scrutiny as a useful guide in our search for integrity. For many, the golden rule has stood for millennia as the ultimate indicator of appropriate behavior when interacting with other people. The question is, how useful is the golden rule as a governor of behavior in the competitive world of business?

The golden rule seems to have something to do with being fair. When you were a youngster, how often did you hear another child cry out, "That's not fair!"? Children are particularly sensitive about what is unfair. Sometimes they complain that other children have violated the understood rules of a game—and frequently follow the complaint with the whine, "I'm telling." Other times they use the complaint to demand something they want when their parents have told them they can't have it—a new toy, more candy, or five more minutes of television at bedtime.

Many times the charge of "unfair" clearly is legitimate: Generally someone has violated a well-established rule or has been inconsistent in its application. For example, in soccer, touching the ball with your hands—unless you are a goalkeeper or you are putting the ball in play from out of bounds—is against the rules, and if a referee does not make the call when it happens, the opposing team will insist that it's unfair, even if it was accidental—especially if they have been called on it and the other team hasn't. The rule is very explicit and should be consistently applied.

Other times, the rules are not as explicitly stated or formally established, but people who are placed at a disadvantage because of a behavior develop a keen sense about its fairness. For example, it seems unfair if a bigger child pushes or bullies a smaller child, or if an older child takes advantage of a younger child in bargaining for things with trickery, or if one child gets to stay up later than another child. Equity seems to be integrally important to fairness—each child should get the same size piece of cake, or a toy of similar perceived value, or the same amount of time with the controls to the video game.

Identifying the rules in gaming ethics is further confounded by the fact that what is considered "proper behavior" is constantly evolving. Sometimes it seems that fair vs. unfair behavior is a moving target, that mores are built on shifting sands. Within my lifespan, there was a time when a bank that advertised was considered sleazy; it was not in keeping with that institution's image of integrity. Even more recently, it was taboo for professionals such as lawyers, CPAs, and physicians to advertise. And certainly no one would actually use a competitor's name in advertising or say anything to denigrate a specific competitor. Over the years, though, the daring in each profession pushed the edges of the "prohibited" (that which was up against the ethical line) long enough to demonstrate the value of this questionable conduct for entrepreneurial success. Gradually others indulged more and more until these things, once taboo, are now just part of doing business.

The "code," however, is still evolving. Some lawyers have printed actual amounts of money they have won for a client in their advertisements, arguing that as long as it is the "truth" there is nothing wrong with doing that. Other lawyers who advertise decry the practice. "It is inappropriate and sleazy . . . we never mention dollar amounts. I won't allow it," says lawyer Ned Siegfried.[7] So we see that in business what is proper ethical behavior is not only unclear but is a changing standard, adding to the difficulty of knowing what is right and what is wrong.

Sometimes discrepancies are not weighed so carefully. For instance, in basketball, it is not unfair for one player to be consistently taller or more talented than another—as long as the teams are in the same league—even though height and talent give an advantage in competition.

In the adult world, people are often stumped by what is fair or unfair. Rules and laws can be complex, inconsistently applied, or even unknown, unwritten, or nonexistent. But, generally, ethical people are considered "fair," and unethical people are "unfair." The label is frequently given with much unclarity.

Terms such as "fair play," "level playing field," and "equal opportunity" are frequently used by people in the world of business. For example, many American companies have complained that Japanese businesses are unfair because they sell their goods in the United States for less than American companies can produce them. And, when Americans have sued or lobbied Congress for trade barriers, Japanese companies have called the American businesses unfair for forcing customers to pay higher prices for Japanese-made products that are made at a cheaper cost than American products. In other situations, employees often complain about "unfair" labor and hiring practices that favor or discriminate against certain groups. Or, companies in the same industry accuse other companies of sneaky marketing and advertising practices, price fixing, or other unfair competitive tactics.

Everyone seems to have a strong sense of what is "fair" and what is "unfair" from their own perspective, but there seem to be very few commonly accepted standards for measuring fairness.

Fairness can be divided into two general categories: first, instances when specific and well-established rules and understanding exist, and second, when no rules or precedents exist. In the business world, we find many practices that are governed by long-established codes, such as: Competitors must not collude with each other in setting prices or engage in "insider trading." When people are found engaging in these practices, they can be prosecuted. The people who are caught in these practices generally knew what they were doing and knew it was wrong, or at least they knew going in that, if caught, a penalty would result, and they understood the risks. In basketball, for instance, a player might deliberately commit a foul to stop another player from shooting a game-winning basket late in the game, but knows that the foul will likely be called by a referee. It's simply a strategic move, though ethically questionable.

However, things get tricky when no guidelines exist or their application becomes inconsistent. In these cases, people are often accused of unfair practices when the practices are uncommon or not understood. We probably cannot expect to rid ourselves of such controversies because we will always have standards or rules that are not agreed upon or not applied universally.

Certainly, "just live the golden rule" is great moral advice for anyone on any occasion. It's the essence of human goodness and the foundation of trust. But, living in a competitive world is the reality most of us face and remains one of the greatest challenges to our belief system. Under the golden rule, "a good [ethical] person is concerned with and responsible for the well-being of others."[8] So, for people in business, living the golden rule is like turning into a fish—virtually impossible. Just consider the question for a moment: How can we be concerned about and accept responsibility for the well-being of others when our individual success is often driven by how we *compare* with others such as competitors, co-workers, etc., and when the motto of the entire business community is either "look out for yourself" (translated: "make a profit for myself") or "enhance stockholder value" (translated as "make a profit for the company"). This conflict of interests prevents anyone who is serious about both business and the treatment of others to successfully fill both roles.

Still, many people believe that competition and the golden rule are compatible. These people may want to do some rethinking: If the object of competition is to beat someone else, or be better, or to put someone else down, is this the golden rule? In sports at least we can say, "It's just a game," but when we're talking about someone's reputation, career, workplace, or family's standard of living, we can't be so casual or flippant.

Once while I was eating breakfast with the CEO of a Fortune 500 company, I asked how he was able to reconcile the competitive world with the golden rule. Without hesitation he said, "I don't." I admire that answer. At least he is honest with himself instead of trying to deceive himself and others that taking customers from a competitor is, somehow, living the golden rule.

■ DON'T DISCARD GOLDEN RULE

Recognizing the difficulty, or impossibility, of applying the golden rule in competitive business, but knowing it can elevate the morality of any society, what should be done?

- 1. Ignore. Do as my CEO friend does—don't even try to reconcile the dilemma.
- 2. Compartmentalize. Make a conscious choice to follow gaming ethics for business and personal ethics in your private life. This raises problems for integrity in which one of the key elements is wholeness or consistency in a person's life. This is not a perfect world. In other areas of our lives we compartmentalize. Perfect integrity (consistency) is probably impossible. A person of integrity is one found to be striving in the direction of consistency.
- 3. Talk. Under any circumstances discuss the challenges with your team. Keep alive the desire for integrity by discussing specific cases like Ted Rockwell and the Wal-Mart pricing case that follows.

WHATEVER THE MARKET WILL BEAR

Actually, our private enterprise system has an answer for this pricing dilemma. We call it "supply and demand." It is an economic system driven by competition and gaming ethics, not by the golden rule. In this system, suppliers offer to sell their products at a certain price. Those who are willing to pay the price make the purchase, which acknowledges the fair exchange of value. Those who are unwilling to pay the price do not make the purchase, so nothing unfair occurs. And, if suppliers can't make a sale at a certain price, they will reduce the price until a fair exchange occurs. So, "fair price" is simply whatever the market will bear. In a market economy, then, there is no such thing as a "fair" or "unfair" price. Whatever people are willing to pay is fair.

Some people, out of a sense of morality, may want to change the system. The communists tried such a system, and over the course of about seventy years, failed. The socialists are still trying to make a new system work. But, the people who believe that the market system is the fairest way to set prices say it's just a matter of economics—not morality. To them, whenever you insert ethics or morality into the mix you are changing to an inefficient system. So to expect everyone to live by the golden rule in a market economy is, perhaps, expecting too much.

- **4.** Avoid self-delusion. The temptation is to devise words and phrases that can lead people to believe they are abiding by the golden rule when they are not. Self-delusion is not integrity.

■ BUSINESS ETHICS: AN AMORAL, THIRD SET

Besides these two major sets of ethics, businesspeople may want to consider one more set of ethical standards, "business ethics." This set can also be called "ethics for profit" or "amoral ethics." The well-known economist Milton Friedman hinted at this set of rules when he said that the primary responsibility of business is to increase its profits, suggesting that the rules are actually amoral, not *im*moral.[9] According to the dictionary, *amoral* is defined as "outside the sphere of morality, non-moral."[10]

Basically, this position suggests that businesses should abide by the laws of the land, but beyond that should not be held to a typical moral code. Instead, they should be held responsible for making a profit—period. This responsibility requires businesses to abide by economic rules, not moral standards, and has little or nothing to do with morals at all. If projecting the image of high moral standards helps the bottom line, that strategy is legitimate. Nevertheless, in business ethics, management follows a standard of personal ethics, but only because it produces economic results, not because it's the right thing to do. Management may give to charities because the act of charity enhances the company's image, which results in winning more customers and improving profits—not because management has a moral obligation to do so.

Morality re-enters when the profits are passed on to shareholders, who then have a personal responsibility to do morally appropriate things with their money based on personal ethics. But as business ethics are amoral, businesses themselves should not be governed by a moral code except to make a profit, so long as it stays within the rules of the game.

The company that aspires to be an institution of integrity is undertaking no simple or small task. It is a challenge of the highest order to just identify the difference between right and wrong, let alone live it.

Now we understand that a possible three sets of rules govern people at work. Decide which set of rules you will follow at which times, and then discuss your philosophy with others to increase agreement and awareness. Then stick to your belief system, applying the different rules to the appropriate situations as you have committed, in both word and deed.

Don't let yourself get caught in the same trap as those executives who advocate personal ethics in their public speeches and statements but then deliberately practice gaming ethics. For example, how often do some senior executives stress truthfulness and high moral standards in their talk but then spend hours with their managers huddling over the annual report to stockholders, trying to manipulate the words so that bad financial news does not show or appears to be unimportant? Or how often do some corporations restate their gift-giving policies at Christmastime—"We remind all employees that it is strictly against company policy for any employee to accept gifts from suppliers, either at work or at home"—while, at the same time, the sales department is updating its list of important clients to whom will be sent impressive gifts "to show our thanks for your business"?

One CEO I know warned his executive team, "If I catch any one of you so much as accepting a free lunch from a supplier or potential supplier, you will be fired." Yet this same CEO continues to supply his salespeople with generous expense accounts to buy lunches and entertainment tickets for his own customers and potential customers.

This duplicity sends conflicting messages to employees: "We practice personal ethics when dealing with our suppliers—lest we find ourselves obligated in some way—while we practice gaming ethics with our customers—making sure they make the 'right' decision." Wouldn't it show more integrity to just openly acknowledge that business is a game and that using gaming ethics is the proper way to play? Let's at least be honest with ourselves.

On the other hand, what would happen if your organization decided to operate within the realm of personal ethics while all the other companies in your industry chose to play by gaming ethics or an amoral set of business ethics? You would place yourself at a serious competitive disadvantage as others would take advantage of all the rules would allow.

Or wouldn't you be placing yourself at risk by choosing to play by gaming ethics when others are playing by personal ethics? You could be left wide open to charges of overstepping the ethical line, and you or your employees might occasionally cross over the legal line, too, and get caught.

And what if you decide to do what others in your industry are doing? If that means follow personal ethics, wonderful; we're all in heaven and we're all rich, too, right? But if everyone is playing by gaming ethics, and especially if we get to be good at it, we subject ourselves to the weak moral stance of "everybody's doing it," and risk jumping or being pushed across the legal lines right into jail or other heavy penalties. After all, even sports teams and their key players get suspended, fined, ejected, penalized, etc. It's more damaging to careers and livelihoods in the business world.

■ **SO WHAT SHOULD WE DO?**

Here are five suggestions to help you wrestle with this multiple-standard dilemma.

1) Acknowledge to yourself that at least two sets of ethical standards, both accepted and legitimate, govern people's actions in the world of business. You may even consider the third set, an amoral variety of "business ethics."
2) Decide tentatively which set generally applies to your organization and industry, after thinking through the implications of embracing each one.
3) Discuss the concepts with others. Make sure everyone understands the different options, independent of your beliefs. Then share opinions and together explore the implications of pursuing each path. Reach a group agreement on a common approach.
4) Implement the decision: make known and put into action your chosen standard.
5) Review your group's progress in establishing the chosen set of rules periodically. Explore the problems, barriers, difficulties, and rewards that surface as a result of choosing to play by this particular set of rules.

Rex had been a top accounting student at the university he attended, and had received several outstanding job offers before he graduated. He accepted a position with a nationally recognized financial firm and soon began to impress his employer. He was highly regarded by the clients he served, and his employer gave him unprecedented opportunities and advancements faster than most people who worked at the firm.

However, for some time Rex had been considering going out on his own and becoming his own boss. After four years with the firm, he decided it was time to make his move. He had gained a great deal of valuable experience, had established a solid reputation in the business community, and now had many valuable contacts. After carefully laying out his plans, he gave his firm two weeks' notice, then set out on his own. The risks of his entrepreneurial venture were soon moderated when he found that several of the firm's clients were willing to switch to him for their financial services. Financially, his first year on his own was much more successful than he had expected.

QUESTIONS

1. Did Rex act ethically? How did he? In what ways did he not?

2. Is "stealing clients" simply a matter of competitive gaming ethics, or is it unethical?

3. Does it make a difference whether Rex enticed the firm's clients to switch or the clients volunteered?

4. Should Rex have let his firm know about his plans when he began to think about going out on his own, or was withholding such information just part of the competitive game?

5. What could Rex's employer have done to show where it stood on this?

DEVELOP THE
ESSENTIAL SKILLS
FOR PERSONAL
INTEGRITY

CHAPTER SEVEN

Integrity Requires Skills

"Intention is not enough. The honest man suspects himself always. He knows honesty is a skill that must be exercised always. Most of us want to be honest, few know how."

S. Leonard Rubenstein[1]

MANY PEOPLE seem to think that the only thing needed for honesty is the desire to be honest. According to this logic, the cause of dishonesty is simply that people desire to be dishonest, so if someone is dishonest, it is because they are being so willfully and consciously, which means, to correct the backward slide of morality in our society, we just need to motivate more people to want to be honest. Furthermore, they believe as long as people are truly sincere, then they are honest as well.

But heartfelt sincerity and the simple desire to be honest by themselves *do not* make people into honest, truth-telling saints. Someone may sincerely believe that the world is flat, but no matter how earnest and heartfelt the claim, it is still an untruth—a lie. A salesperson many convince himself or herself to sincerely believe that the company's product is, indeed, the best product on the market, or a broker may sincerely believe that there is no downside risk to the investment he or she is selling, but that belief alone does not make it true.

Some people are uncomfortable equating speaking an untruth with lying. They believe that when someone passes on an untruth not knowing their statement is false, it does not make them a liar; they believe that ignorance is a defense against lying. But a person really conscious of integrity does not use being uninformed as a psychological defense. On the contrary, as Leonard Rubenstein, chairman of the English Department at Pennsylvania State University, says, "The honest man suspects himself always." This attitude of positive concern produces different behavior than a casual one does, where a person is prone to just shrugging their shoulders and saying, "I just didn't know."

Too many of us are like Leah Solowsky, a typical high school sophomore over-burdened with "a ton of homework" and faced with an assignment to write an essay on healthy eating in Spanish. She thought of her computer and the Internet.

> Solowsky cruised to the Alta Vista search engine, clicked on "Spanish," and typed in "la dieta." Fifteen minutes later, she had everything she needed to know about fruits, vegetables, and grains—all in flawless español. She quickly retyped the information and handed in her paper the next day. "I had a ton of homework, I wasn't doing well in the class, and I felt hey, this is one way to boost my grade," explains Solowsky, now a junior with a B-plus average at the highly competitive Gulliver Preparation School in Miami. "I didn't think it was cheating, because I didn't even stop to think about it."[2]

The point is, people working to be honest *do* think about such things. People of integrity have a consciousness that causes them to raise questions about the validity of information they are passing on. People who approach honesty casually just don't give it much thought. This casual attitude about truthfulness and honesty can cause substantial pain, and in the end, the claimed innocence, "but I didn't know," does little to ease the pain and damage.

■ SCAMMED BY GOOD INTENTIONS

Several years ago an insurance salesman set about to persuade me to convert my almost-paid-up life-insurance policy to a new, improved policy. Instead of hold-ing $20,000 in paid-for insurance, this new plan would provide me with up to $40,000 of paid-for insurance without any additional cost. When I pressed the salesman about the possible downside risks to this changeover, he assured me that changes in interest rates could possibly reduce the policy's value to $34,000 or $32,000, but I would still be way ahead of the $20,000 face value I currently had. The agent seemed so sincere, convincing, and confident that I accepted his proposal to improve my financial position. Obviously, I reasoned, he is a trustworthy person. I felt he really believed that what he was telling me was the truth. Besides, he represented a reputable and trustworthy firm.

A few years after the conversion, I began to receive premium notices from the insurance company. When I called my agent, he comforted me by saying, "Just let it go. It will build up a little debt of 'premium due' that will reduce your final face value a bit, possibly as far as the $34,000 or so that I mentioned could happen. But you will still be way ahead."

After another two or three years the debt of premium due was building up so fast I began to worry that, unless I died pretty soon, I could end up with no insurance at all. I called my agent and expressed the concern I had about losing my financial nest egg. He told me that interest rates had changed so much it was hard to predict what could happen, but that losing the principal amount was, indeed, a risk. "But," I said, "you assured me that I would still be left with $32,000 to $34,000 in insurance face value, even with the declining interest rates."

"Well," he responded, "you can't always predict these things, even though we were very confident at the time that the assurances we gave you about the range of possible risk fluctuations were valid."

"So, what do I do now?" I asked. "Do I just wait until all my face value disappears?"

"You could live with that possibility, hoping interest rates will turn around," he said. "Or, you could convert back to what you had before with a locked-in, paid-up value."

"If I did that, how much insurance would I have?" I asked.

"I'll calculate that for you and get back to you," he promised. He did get back to me. Instead of the $20,000 of original insurance, I now had $16,000. Although I knew he had likely been motivated by the commissions he would gain by converting my insurance, I also believe that he had been truly sincere about the promises he made. Nevertheless, his sincerity and belief about how much the conversion would benefit me did not make it so.

Sincerity does not an honest person make. Desire and motivation do not produce truth tellers. To put it bluntly, a sincere person can still be a blatant liar.

■ THE ESSENTIAL SKILLS OF HONESTY

Besides the desire or motivation to be honest, it takes highly developed and finely honed skills to be a truth teller. Telling the truth is not a natural, innate instinct that simply abides dormantly in all of us, only waiting to come out. It is more like a skill, like mastering the piano, operating a computer, playing tennis, cooking, or performing a financial analysis.

Beginning piano players do not simply express the will to become great concert pianists and then set out immediately to arrange concert bookings for the following weekend. Such expectations are ridiculous to even think about. Although top piano players must begin with a strong desire to master their talent, they must still apply great effort, often over the course of many years, to develop the skills necessary to become concert performers. They must first learn the concepts, theories, and principles of music. They must learn the fine nuances of stroking the keys in different ways to create different tones and dynamics, and to evoke different feelings in their listeners. They must learn the elements of composition and the different styles and tonal qualities of various pianos. Such knowledge doesn't come from attending a one-day seminar by a professional piano teacher who urges you to become a good pianist. It comes from extensive personal study and practice. It involves testing different ideas, theories, and principles in the effort to find your own individual voice in the art form and then selecting the best way to combine all the elements in the most effective way for different audiences.

To extend the metaphor even further, even though the *desire* to become a concert pianist can be equal in two different people, the *results* can be quite unequal, depending upon several elements, including the amount and quality of practice and instruction. The desire of one person may lead them to search out the best instruction and apply rigorous discipline and practice routine, resulting in great piano techniques and critical acclaim. Another person may get poor advice and guidance, learn faulty or limiting techniques, or engage in practice habits that result only in mediocre renditions, and therefore never get the same results as the first person. The second person may impress any group of friends with a jazzed-up version of "Chopsticks," but when faced with more complex music, he or she could only blunder through it haphazardly without any sense of dynamics.

So it is with truth telling. The people who are willing to put in the effort to develop the skills of an honest person are more likely to become expert truth tellers than those who fail to recognize the necessity of cultivating those skills, or those who recognize the need but fail to develop the skills. As a result, many of us are like the person who claims to be an expert piano player, but who only has the skill to play "Chopsticks." We claim to be truth tellers, but we have only developed the skills for a very basic level of performance. When circumstances are simple (we call them "black and white," "right and wrong," "cut and dry") we can express the truth very efficiently. But when we face more complicated situations—the so-called gray areas—we become major blunderers. For many, this condition is worsened by the often-unconscious attitude, "I am an honest person, so what I do and say is honest." This attitude blocks out even the idea that skills are needed to be honest, let alone the idea that the necessary skill development requires concerted effort. We end up saying and doing things that have little resemblance to truth or honesty, without even meaning to.

Good piano playing requires many skills: hand-eye coordination; hand dexterity; a sense of rhythm; the ability to read music, distinguish different pitches, transpose keys; and so on. Likewise, several skills are needed for the art of honesty. There are two general skills: First, the ability to *determine* what is truth and what is not. Second, the ability to *convey* that truth.

■ I. SKILLS FOR DETERMINING THE TRUTH

It seems obvious that we would be hard-pressed to tell the truth unless we were aware of what the truth were. Many people who desire to be serious truth tellers often blunder and fall short because they have not developed the necessary skills for determining the truth of a matter. Like piano playing, this is not *a* skill but a combination of sub-skills.

THE SKILL AND WILL OF INQUIRY

Inquiry is "to investigate—to make a careful study of [a thing] in order to discover the facts about it."[3] This skill must be applied not only on information received from others but also on our own ideas—observations and conclusions we draw on our own must be probed with inquiry, too.

This skill of inquiry is necessary to avoid three common hazards that bring down the unwary truth teller.

- **1. The inclination to accept without question ideas that reinforce our own opinions and perceptions.** When an executive has made up her mind that a merger is a good deal, she is prone to accept and use any data that confirms her predetermined idea, often without confirmation. The skill of inquiry enables her to raise probing questions about the data: where did it come from? Who said it? Is it complete? Often this act of self-inquiry requires as much will as it does skill. The willingness and ability to question even data that affirms a person's own beliefs—political, economic, or personal—is a mark of a person of integrity.

- **2. The inclination to perceive selectively, as described in Chapter One.** Even when a person is given "all the facts," selective perception causes them to see and remember only those facts that reinforce their perceptions, and ignore or forget those facts that threaten their ideas. In the insurance incident described earlier, the agent was inclined to hear and remember his company's financial analyst's statements that held promise of increased value ($40,000 for me) and tended to downgrade, ignore, or minimize those statements that said it was not a sure thing. Then he passed that message on to me.

  Selective perception can give you the illusion that you are exercising inquiry because you are able to cite specific data points. Our personal filtering process can cause serious violations of the truth, but when you add to that the similar filtering that has probably occurred several times before it arrived at your mental doorstep, the dangers of this trap are compounded. Quite like the parlor game of whisper—passing a message around a circle one person at a time—seldom is the end message what it was at the beginning. This is why serious truth tellers use the skill of inquiry to trace a piece of information back to its original source whenever possible—even with ideas they want to be true.

- **3. The tendency to treat conclusions as facts.** It is surprising how natural it is for people to fill in the visual or verbal blanks to complete a picture or idea. Notice how an artist can stroke a few simple lines and the viewer will complete the picture of a face, or a cat, or a mountain in their minds. A writer or a speaker does the same with words like "a tranquil stream flowed through the meadow." Listeners or readers fill in the grass, trees, and sunshine in their minds. The positive side to this practice of completing the picture or drawing conclusions without all the detail frequently facilitates communication and makes it efficient. When it comes to discerning the truth, however, this habit can entrap people in an untruth that they convey to someone else as a truth.

  An example is Robert Frost's poem "Mending Wall." He describes how he and his neighbor replace the stones annually that have fallen from the rock wall (fence) between their properties. Twice the phrase "good fences make good neighbors" appears in the writing. Most people not familiar with the poem readily fill in the message, concluding that Frost advocates the virtues of fences. Inquiry would reveal that Frost has serious criticism of how fences tend to isolate neighbors from one another, and that he uses the phrase in a context of sarcasm.

Treating conclusions as facts occurs in a three-step process. An incident happens. We make observations. We draw conclusions.

INCIDENT → OBSERVATIONS → CONCLUSIONS

People often fail to determine the truth because they lock onto some conclusion, or opinion, and then treat that conclusion as a fact or as the truth. Consider this example:

What happened to John?

> John was walking along slowly. He looked down, saw a hole in his suit, and in a few minutes, he was dead.

I have tried this example with many groups in a classroom setting. You may want to try it on your workgroup. Many people are quick to respond with their conclusions, speaking as though the facts are obvious: He was shot. When I push for other possibilities, I might hear, "He was stabbed," "He had a heart attack," "He wasn't watching and was hit by a bus"—all conclusions from an imagined street setting.

Serious truth tellers develop their questioning skills, either silently in the mind or out loud. Sometimes a person with a skill for inquiry speaks up. If not, I begin the process.

"Why was John walking along slowly?"

They reason, conclude, envision: he was old, or tired, or just being thoughtful, still clinging to the street scene as though that were a fact.

Up to this point, most have concluded—accepted as fact—that the suit with the hole was one with a shirt and tie. I inquire, "What are we assuming about John's suit?" Someone says, "It could be a space suit . . . or a diving suit," and this sparks whole new images about what the truth may be and encourages further inquiry.

Why was John walking along slowly? Anyone who has tried to walk with water up to their chest understands. How did John die? Shot? It is possible he drowned.

These inquiry skills are necessary to penetrate barriers to determining truth such as benign neglect. In life generally, and corporate life particularly, learning the truth about dishonest behavior is especially challenging. This occurs because the pressure to meet a goal (say a profit goal) creates incremental morality, which feeds the dishonesty balloon, which goes unnoticed until it explodes. Exercising the skill of inquiry could nip this process in the bud. Why doesn't it?

To do this requires, at times, very serious questioning and probing to find out the truth of what is happening. However, the energy and attention required to produce, say, that 19 percent growth rate, or secure the merger, or close the large contract does not leave enough energy or time to apply the skill of inquiry. Also, but not just charging ahead no matter what, the inquirer can be distracted from the goal of 19 percent growth. To be successful at it, you will need to admit up-front that it can dampen the momentum and enthusiasm needed to achieve the desired goal.

Benignly neglecting to find the truth is a better explanation for most corporate dishonesty than are accusations of deliberate lying.

JUST FOR PRACTICE

Communications Company A advertises "long distance calls only $0.04 a minute." A naive customer concludes, "What a deal! My telephone company charges $0.14 a minute." If the customer would inquire a bit further he or she would learn the monthly fee for the system is $29.99 plus $0.04 a minute. Which means if one did just ten minutes of calls a month it would actually cost $3.03 a minute. Even if the person made 100 minutes of calls, it would cost $0.33 a minute.

Honest people must develop the skill to recognize that *conclusions* are not *facts*. They acknowledge to themselves that other conclusions are possible, and they humbly admit to themselves, "My conclusions may not be right. I'd better search for more information." The ability to envision alternate conclusions is one of the sub-skills that enhances the skill of inquiry and raises us above the "Chopsticks" level of truth telling.

The second general skill necessary for being an honest person, is the capacity to *convey* the truth once it has been identified. Conveying the truth is an even greater challenge than determining it. This skill involves a good communicator's every ability and sensitivity. In American society, the skill of using the language to persuade, motivate, and induce has been developed to a very high art. However, the ability to convey truth so that it is clearly and rightly understood by others has not had nearly so much focus, hence, has not been refined to such a fine skill. Remember, skilled truth tellers are not just concerned with stating the facts, but also with conveying a true impression. There are so many techniques and elements that the communicator can combine for the total effect: word selection, tone of voice, facial expression, body language, actions, silence, visuals, color, the printed word, and more.

Words alone give a very interesting challenge, even if everyone agreed on their meaning—which they don't. Even a word as simple and familiar as *sale*—what does it mean? Reduced prices? Or just come in and buy?

"An incredible deal," "Going out of business," "Overstocked," "40% off" (off what?) certainly mean something different for the buyer than for the seller. One important attribute of integrity is being forthright: straightforward, frank, candid. The clever selection and cunning phrasing of words may sell goods and services or reinforce a desired corporate image, but is not the mark of integrity.

"Blue book price." For years I had heard the phrase and understood it to be the industry's standard of value for each car. Reassuring to a buyer? Later the owner of a dealership told me there are at least three blue book prices, one for buying, one for selling, and one for wholesale. So what does "blue book" mean? What does the dealer hope it means?

IT'S ALL SEMANTICS

I remember having a conversation with the professor who supervised my doctoral thesis. I had used the word peer in my writing, and he wanted me to clarify my meaning. He said, "Don't you really mean 'equal' rather than 'peer'?"

I responded, "That's exactly what I mean." But somehow in his mind the word peer meant "superior" or "mentor," not an equal or someone at the same level. Words can and do have different technical and emotional meanings for different people. Even when people agree on meaning, the language can be misleading.

I have seen "customized intelligence" and "industrial research" used to describe competitive espionage or spying.

"Fiscal adjustments" used to describe major cuts in budget.

"Reorganization" or "downsizing" are terms used to disguise layoffs.

"Spin" is a frequently used euphemism for "misleading" or "deceit."

Until sales of XYZ Co. compared to industry
average in 100's (2002)

Until sales of XYZ Co. compared to industry
average in 100's (2002)

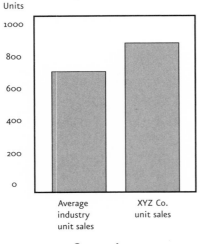

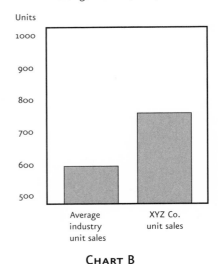

CHART A

CHART B

WHAT YOU SEE

The use of visuals is supposedly intended to help make things clearer. Not just printed statements and pictures, but also "hard-fact data graphs." Above is a bar graph showing the XYZ Company's unit sales compared to the industry's average. Which chart would you select for the annual report of XYZ Co.?

A casual glance at Chart B gives the impression that XYZ Co. is doing much better vis-à-vis the industry than Chart A, but a close study reveals that they show exactly the same 600,000-unit average sales for the industry and 800,000-unit sales for XYZ Co. The difference is just a matter of starting with a different baseline—500 rather than 0. There is nothing illegal with the device used in Chart B, nor does it violate any rules, but is it honest? Does it convey a true impression?

The communicator has so many devices available, some very subtle. When you are aware of this challenge, you can become skilled and able to make the extra effort needed to make sure that a true impression is conveyed.

The neophyte or unskilled truth teller will often become defensive: "I stated the situation clearly. It's not my fault if they don't understand English." Then they meticulously review each word to justify that it was not their fault they were misunderstood. On the other hand, people who are skilled in honesty have learned to be sensitive to recognize, through body language, facial expressions, and verbal responses, that listeners may be getting the wrong impression. Then they skillfully review and clarify until they are confident that recipients have received a true understanding.

How often, after a manager has instructed a group on some matter, does she conclude with, "Do you understand?" or "Now is it clear to everyone what this new policy is?" When the queries are met with silence or nods, the manager usually assumes they do understand. She is right—they do. The question is *what* do they understand? Many undoubtedly understand exactly what was intended, but others may understand something different. Here, a manager skilled in communication will invite feedback to determine what was understood: "In your words, tell me what you now understand."

People at the "Chopsticks" level worry only that they have made a defendable statement they can use later to protect themselves with. They do

> The skill of communication is so nuanced that one can unintentionally seriously mislead others even with small notes. The story is told of J. Edgar Hoover, the long-time director of the FBI, who, one day after reviewing a draft of a memo he had dictated to his secretary to be sent to his field agents, noted in the margin, "Watch the borders." The secretary typed up the finished memo and sent it out. For two weeks there was a heightened concentration of agents along the United States borders. The director's penciled note had been intended as instruction to the secretary about the margins on the paper when typing up the memo, not about the country's borders.

not understand that the obligation of truly honest people is not only to make correct statements but also to test and make sure those statements are properly understood. Skilled truth tellers are sensitive to what is being understood, not just what is being said. So, the truth is often sacrificed because, even though people desire to be honest, they blunder due to the lack of skills to convey a true impression.

■ THE DELIBERATE MISUSE OF COMMUNICATIONS SKILLS

On the other hand, some people who possess the skills to convey a true impression deliberately misuse those skills. Great persuaders are frequently guilty of using these skills to mislead or to swindle rather than to convey a true impression. They are so eager to win a prize, make a sale, win an election, or win an argument that they become very skilled at abiding by the letter of the law while still conveying a wrong impression. Clever wordsmiths, image makers, and advertisers are very skilled at this.

Years ago, I cut out a cartoon that showed a man driving his recently purchased used-car back into the lot with a look of serious disappointment on his face. Above the entrance was a sign that read, "Guaranteed Used Cars." In the caption, the lot manager was explaining, "You misinterpreted the sign: We guarantee the cars to be used." The skills for conveying true impressions are also used cleverly to entrap.

People are often told to read the fine print before signing a contract. Why? What is there in the fine print? We all know that people generally overlook the fine print. Even if they do read it, they generally don't understand it, or they conclude it must not be very important or else it would be in large print.

The failure to convey the truth or the deliberate attempt to distort the truth occurs in oral communication as well as written. Recently, over the radio, I have heard advertisements that encourage people to invest in commodities that are generally regarded as high-risk investments, such as heating oil. During most of the sixty-second advertisement, the speaker paints a glowing picture of how you can leverage $5,000 into $20,000 in just a few short months. Other similar ads declare that you can earn 100 percent a month on your investment. In the last five or ten seconds of these ads, the voice speaks so fast that it's almost impossible to hear, let alone discern what is being said. The voice mumbles quick phrases like, "This return is not guaranteed; you could lose all your investment," and other statements designed to meet the technical requirements of the law, but that certainly don't meet the requirements of being a skillful truth teller—they surely don't convey a true impression. In this case, the most important thing for investors to know would be that these are very high-risk investments, but the impression conveyed is that everyone will have great opportunities for quick wealth without any but a little risk. (At the end of one of the ads, one advertiser cynically comments, "Oh, the lawyers make us put this in . . ." Then quickly, as though it were unimportant, the qualifications and limitations are routinely stated like some monotone and pedantic bureaucratic poetry.)

Every businessperson must recognize that desire and good intentions alone do not make a person or a company honest. To be an effective truth teller, you must acquire and practice the proper skills. You must be able to distinguish what is true from what is false, and be able to convey the truth.

For several days there had been talk around the Pacific factory floor that a larger company was planning to buy out Pacific Manufacturing Company. Pacific supplied parts to many large manufacturers and assemblers, and the company employed nearly 300 people.

The foreman of one of the departments began to be concerned about the rumors because of the effect they were having on employee morale. After listening to the rumors for several days, the foreman decided to get to the heart of the matter. While things seemed to be going smoothly on the floor, he quietly slipped away to the superintendent's office on the second floor of the administrative section of the building. When the secretary ushered him into his boss's office, the foreman closed the door and sat down. After relating to the superintendent the talk he had been hearing on the factory floor, the foreman asked, "I just need to know, is there any truth to these rumors?"

The superintendent knew that negotiations had been underway for a possible buyout. And just that morning he had been in the president's office, where he had been given strict instructions to "keep this absolutely quiet. In the next two days, we will be in very sensitive negotiations, so 'mum's' the word. Flatly deny that any talks are going on if you have to." So according to his instructions and faithfulness to the trust the president had placed in him, the superintendent told the foreman, "There isn't going to be a buyout. You know that there will always be rumors going around in this industry. This is just more groundless talk."

The foreman returned to his crew and during a coffee break explained that he had investigated the rumors: there would be no buyout of Pacific Manufacturing Company.

Three days later, it was publicly announced, "A successful merger has been negotiated between Pacific Manufacturing Company and General Systems, Inc. The owners and management of both companies are pleased with the arrangements. The Pacific Manufacturing plant will take on the name of the other company, but otherwise it is expected that company operations will continue as they have in the foreseeable future."

1. If you were the foreman, how would you feel? What would you do?

2. Did the foreman tell an untruth? Was it a lie? Does the sincerity with which he spoke to his crew make him a truth teller?

3. Can a person be sincere and still lie?

4. Was the foreman a skilled truth teller? How could he have exercised more skill at finding out the truth? How could he have been more skillful at conveying his message to the crew?

RESOLVE CONFLICTS OF PRINCIPLE: THERE ARE NO GRAY AREAS

CHAPTER EIGHT

Principles in Conflict

IN 1974, in the NATO Defense Organization, a major decision was being made about which fighter plane would be used by the military organization. Analysis and debate centered mainly around two new American-designed planes: Northrop's F-17 and General Dynamics' F-16. The French-built Mirage F-1 was also in the running. After all the performance tests and analysis of the cost of manufacturing and cost of operation, most people involved felt the F-16 was significantly better. The French, however, still held out for their own machine.

One member of the decision team was Paul Stehlin, a high-ranking French Air Force officer who had been commander of the Air Force under Charles de Gaulle. When a reporter asked him for his opinion about the best choice, Stehlin said that in his honest judgment, the American-made F-16 was superior. After he made the public statement, the French Air Force promptly retired him from service for his "unpatriotic" remarks.[1]

Mr. Stehlin's experience is a common example of another fundamental cause of dishonesty for many members of organizations. Senior executives and the public frequently criticize frontline employees and mid-level managers for being dishonest, but often when employees are honest they are punished, much like the French officer was. This hypocrisy, advocating honesty but rewarding dishonesty, arises because people fail to recognize the intense dilemmas inherent in complete honesty.

Dilemmas of this kind constantly plague businesspeople. Benjamin Selekman, professor of labor relations at Harvard Graduate School of Business, writes that to expect business executives to live the Judeo-Christian ethic places them in a state of perpetual sinfulness; it's impossible to expect managers to obey all the principles of the Judeo-Christian ethic and still keep their jobs.[2]

Frequently in our careers two right principles come in conflict with each other in such a way that it becomes impossible to abide both. For example, most people I know believe in and advocate the principle of honesty. Most of those same people also believe in and advocate the principle of kindness. Most likely you can recall an incident in the recent past where if you would have been honest it would have forced you to be unkind; or when you chose to be kind you were left with the feeling you had not been honest.

■ THERE ARE NO GRAY AREAS

When faced with one of these "impossible" dilemmas, a most common response is, "That's one of those gray areas." Make for yourself a list of principles that create conflicts: e.g., time with family versus time at work and career success, honesty versus effectiveness in producing results, doing what's best for yourself versus what is best for the organization, honesty about fiscal matters versus stockholder value.

Labeling a situation a "gray area" is not only useless in raising moral integrity but also can be harmful to the cause. Using the label leads away from a rational resolution to the dilemma. Calling a situation a "gray area" suggests that it's hard to see what the problem is, or that it's impossible to resolve logically, or that there is no right or wrong answer, so whatever decision is made is okay, "as long as it doesn't hurt me." But the truth is, situations can be made clear even though they may require extensive thought and difficult decisions. When you avoid using the label "a gray area," you accept the challenge of rationally choosing between two right principles.

■ LOYALTY VERSUS HONESTY

In almost all authoritarian organizations—including business—loyalty and honesty are a common and frustrating conflict. Our culture's ethic teaches that people should be honest, but it also teaches that they should be loyal and obedient. The French general faced a conflict between loyalty to his country and honesty—loyalty to his own conscience. Arguing in favor of the French plane might have protected him from the wrath of his fellow citizens and even won their praise, but would have forced him to live with a conscience that reminded him he had not told the truth.

Sometimes people face a conflict between loyalty to one person and loyalty to another. It could be said the French general faced a conflict between loyalty to his country and loyalty to NATO. Again, he could have been loyal to his country and recommended the French plane, but perhaps he recognized a design flaw in the French plane and knew that by recommending it he could jeopardize the safety and maneuverability of NATO pilots in the future, all because he did not give his honest judgment when asked for it. (If he *did* know of such a flaw in the French plane, we could even argue that he *was* loyal to the French Air Force by not pointing out the flaw to the public, but quietly recommending the F-16 instead.)

Loyalty and honesty are frequently in conflict when people are asked to express their judgments about others, particularly when one person is the other person's boss or subordinate.

Adam Collins had worked for the Nary Company for several years. For the past six years, he had been a superintendent under Mike Hannah, the vice president of production. During that time, they had worked together closely, and Adam felt that he knew Mike very well and he liked him very much on a personal level. However, he felt that Mike had become obsolete as a leader.

In the past, Mike had demonstrated technical competence, but he had never been a leader. In fact Adam felt that if it weren't for the experienced superintendents under Mike and their leadership abilities, the company would be having serious difficulty. As it was, the company was holding its own, but it was not nearly as strong as its resources and potential indicated it could be.

One day when Adam was waiting at the corner for the light to change so he could cross Main Street, George Owen, the vice chairman of Nary Company's board, arrived at the corner alongside him. Adam knew Mr. Owen reasonably well through other contacts in the community. After a casual exchange of greetings, Mr. Owen asked, "Adam, I've been wondering about our management team. In your opinion, just how good of a leader do you think Mike Hannah is? Is he giving us the leadership the company needs?" As the light changed, both men began to walk across the street together, and Adam needed to choose between loyalty and honesty.

If you were Adam, with strong desires to be honest, but at the same time wanting to be loyal to Mike Hannah, what would you say to Mr. Owen? Is there a way to answer the question that is both honest and loyal? Remember, "To tell the truth is not just to state the facts, but to convey a true impression."

In such an instance, many people would put on their "political cap" and try to come up with something that is "technically" truthful, or that skirts around the issue but is essentially misleading or disloyal. They would avoid the question by saying, "I'm not sure that's an appropriate question to ask me," or "How do *you* think he is working out?" or "I really like him personally," or change the subject by saying, "Oh, watch out for that car." These are messages of subtle criticism and would not be loyal—"nothing is as damning as faint praise."

George Owen knows Adam—that if Adam thinks highly of his boss, he won't hesitate to say so. So, any hesitation or attempt to maneuver around the question would be understood by Mike as a form of disloyalty if he had been present in the conversation or if he had found out about it later. On the other hand, if Adam decides to react to the question with real loyalty by giving Mike a strong endorsement, it would be dishonest. Such conflicts are relatively common and affect everyone.

"It never should have been that way," many people demand. They believe that if we can just be a bit more patient and calm, we can always find a way to be both loyal and honest if we so desire. Indeed, we would all like to have it both ways. But life is not that way. Conflicts of principles do exist, and we should stop trying to avoid this reality. Recognizing that conflicts of principles exist is the first step in handling one of the major, root causes of dishonesty. This kind of conflict is exactly what induces or traps people into lying—people rarely make an outright decision to lie.

■ WHICH PRINCIPLE COMES FIRST

So, what should we do when faced with such conflicts? How do we decide which principle to abide by and which to violate? Should we be honest or loyal? How do we decide which person or group we should be loyal to, if honesty is not the question? To answer these questions, you must establish a hierarchy of principles.

Now, most people recognize that some things are more important than others. For instance, I think that most people believe it's more important to preserve

CASUALTIES OF WAR

There is intense pressure for people to be loyal to their bosses, especially in the public spotlight. During the Vietnam War, General William Westmoreland was in command of the American forces under President Lyndon B. Johnson. Both were men respected for their reputations of honesty and loyalty. Johnson was under pressure from Congress and the American public to either show that the conflict was leading to an American victory or pull out the troops. He asked General Westmoreland to give evidence of American success. But when Westmoreland asked Colonel Gains Hawkins to produce numbers to back him up, the numbers were never enough to satisfy Johnson that he could convince Congress, let alone the public. After repeatedly revising the numbers, Gains finally could no longer live with his role in the deception.

[General Westmoreland] was trained from the start in accepting and obeying commands. He remained loyal to his own vision, and his definition of loyalty. Therefore when his intelligence officers showed him estimates that reflected the darker reality, he rejected those estimates and demanded that the enemy's troop level be lowered. He did this, I suspect, without even realizing what he was doing.

In 1967, [Colonel Gains] Hawkins was caught between the conflict of two loyalties—the first to the truth as he saw it, and the second to orders from a superior that forced him to doctor his work during a time of war. He had followed the traditional loyalty, gone along with his superiors, and in the process he had begun to feel that he had been untrue to himself.

The true figures he came up with then reflected a lack of American progress. Yet that would be a difficult problem for a president facing a reelection campaign. The first time he brought in the figures, they were rejected so he made them a few percentage points more acceptable . . . and the second time he brought them in they were rejected.

He [Colonel Hawkins] had lost the one thing he prided himself on—his own honesty.

Someone asked what he thought about Westmoreland, and he [Hawkins] said, more in sadness than anger, "He left his honor in the same damn place I left my integrity.[3]

SPEAKING THE TRUTH CAN BE DISLOYAL

One young junior manager of a large retail chain learned this generally unwritten rule the hard way. Alex Sanderson had just been promoted from head clerk to assistant supervisor and had been relocated from Pennsylvania to a new assign-ment in Massachusetts. Each of the chain's stores included a management team that consisted of a manager, a supervisor, an assistant supervisor, and a head clerk. Managers, in addition to their salary, were paid a percentage of store profits, determined after each semiannual physical inventory. Since variations in inventory could impact profits, some managers faced a temptation to "stretch" the rules of inventory to show a greater profit and so increase their bonuses and opportunities for advancement.

After he had been in Massachusetts for several weeks, Alex observed that the store's inventory books were inaccurate and violated company inventory management rules. But when he called this to the manager's attention, the manager told him, "Don't worry, nearly everybody does it this way." But violating company rules weighed upon Alex's mind, and he felt that the manager was being dishonest. The second time he raised his concern, the manager said, "Take care of your own business; I know how to run this store."

Several weeks passed, and Alex began to worry about the dishonest practices of the store manager. Finally, in desperation, he contacted an officer of the company and exposed the store's dishonest inventory methods. After a thorough

(continued on next page)

a person's life than to avoid a lie, if they were forced to choose between the two. And, for many, it's more important to be kind than to be completely honest. But, between honesty and loyalty, which is the higher principle?

A hierarchy of principles can be established for one of two reasons: because our personal convictions require it, or because our organization requires it, whether it is stated explicitly in policy or expressed in its reward-and-punishment system. Hopefully, for our peace of mind, these two will be the same. Be aware, however, that most organizations, and society in general, prefer loyalty over honesty and give it the greater reward.

One successful businessman recalled in his autobiography how he learned the hierarchy of priorities. When he was a young man just starting his career, he had an interview with his mentor, the company owner who had already established his own successful business. The owner asked, "What is the most important characteristic to be successful in business?"

Immediately the young man responded, "Integrity."

"No, it's not," replied the employer. "Loyalty is the most important and always comes first." He later added that integrity was also important. But regardless of which principle was actually more important, by making the statement he firmly established which principle was at the top of the hierarchy for him, and he emphatically announced that whenever the two came into conflict the young man was to choose loyalty.

Only at the peril of their careers will aspiring young employees ignore this basic hierarchy when making decisions between the conflicting principles of loyalty and honesty. Even when they would be speaking out to expose an act of gross wrongdoing, loyalty will still invoke a greater reward.

Telling the truth to expose the wrongdoing of a superior is certainly a perilous step. An excellent book called *Whistle Blowing*, a compilation of famous incidents in which people have exposed gross fraud, shows that time and again, society does not reward the tattletale.[4] Such people find out that no one wants them around because of their questionable loyalty. In our society it is worse to be a "squealer" than to be dishonest. For more on whistle blowing, see Chapter Nine.

Part of the problem is that honesty is rarely rewarded when it is chosen over loyalty. In fact, it is generally punished either formally or in subtle ways. To reduce the personal conflict for people who are not psychologically prepared to suppress their honest opinions, perhaps we should reassure them that being "less than honest" is acceptable when loyalty to the boss or the company is at stake. Then at least we could acknowledge the practice and allow it to continue in the open.

This raises the question, under what circumstances *is* dishonesty in the cause of loyalty acceptable? When the company is profitable and growing? When times are tough? When we would avoid embarrassment to the company? When we want to keep information about our internal difficulties from competitors? When it would precipitate too much new legislation in the industry or force the company to conform to more rigid standards?

Martin Feldstein, chairman of the President's Council of Economic Advisors, realized the consequences of straying from the administration's official line about the consequences of the federal deficit and other budget concerns, although he was not attempting to expose any wrongdoing. He found out publicly that the

---

investigation, the company officer verified Alex's story, and he disciplined the manager.

However, the other members of the store's management team soon found out who had reported the violations and began to alienate Alex. Alex also felt guilty for having been disloyal to the store, and finally he resigned. In the meantime, the officers of the company at headquarters were anxious to retain him, for he was a competent person with good management potential and unusually high standards of honesty. Rather than allow him to resign, the company offered him three months of paid leave so that he could consider a new assignment.

In the meantime, company officers began to inquire to see if any of the chain's stores would accept Alex as an assistant manager. But the company grapevine had already become acquainted with the incident, and as Alex already sensed, no one wanted to take him on because they could not trust his loyalty. Reluctantly, the company let the promising young manager go to pursue his career elsewhere. Ironically, the dishonest manager, though he was disciplined, retained his position as manager (because he had the reputation of being a "profitable manager"), while the honest young man with potential was now unemployed.

administration preferred that he be loyal instead of honest in expressing his professional opinions:

> President Reagan's chief economist still had a job yesterday, but his hold on it appeared to be tenuous.
>
> Martin Feldstein, chairman of Reagan's Council of Economic Affairs, was publicly rebuked by White House officials, who are upset that he has strayed from the official line on such sensitive issues as the budget deficit, tax increases, and defense spending. Larry Peakes, Reagan's chief spokesman, said, "Obviously, the President and Secretary of Treasury don't agree with Mr. Feldstein and are unhappy that the economist has been voicing his differences in a series of recent speeches."
>
> Further, another aide said that the economist's public statements have tainted him with disloyalty and shown him to be "not a team player"—a major sin within any administration.[5]

Some argue that Feldstein's voicing his disagreement in a public speech was his sin, even though he was honest. But what should Feldstein have answered if a reporter had asked for his opinion? Should he have been dishonest and covered up any disagreements he might have been having with the president? Should he simply have said, "No comment," and assumed that no one would take such a response as a subtle statement of disloyalty? Or, should he simply have voiced his opinion? As the reporter indicated, the greater sin in the eyes of society was to be disloyal.

Too often, in my opinion, honesty takes a back seat to loyalty. Expressions of candid thinking, particularly when they are at variance with those in authority, are construed as a lack of loyalty or a display of questionable support, or to somehow mean that the person is not a team player—which means most managers feel that the best team players are the ones who can comfortably suppress their true feelings, conflicting ideas, and candid observations that would not correspond with those of the people in authority. When these employees are asked, "Do you agree?" they can say, "yes" even if they don't agree, and not for a moment feel dishonest about it. In situations when the boss asks, "Let me have your honest opinion," unless our opinions are similar to the chief's, we don't often take the invitation too literally. As a result, businesses do not embrace creative new ideas or challenge their own thinking in an effort to improve themselves. Diversity of thought is subordinated to orthodoxy as interpreted by the boss.

Sometimes loyalty problems center around the difficulty of choosing who to be loyal to and then how to handle the situation, particularly if the choice will require a shifting of loyalties. One senior manager, the executive vice president of a large organization who had kept his position under a succession of several presidents, advised aspiring young subordinates, "Never get involved in controversial matters if you can possibly avoid them." He demonstrated his philosophy a short time later.

When the new president accused a mid-level manager of having made a foolish decision, one of the manager's peers, another mid-level manager, reassured the president that the person's actions had been carried out under the direction and approval of the former president. He also explained that the executive vice president had been in on the decision and could verify the fact. But when the manager's peer turned to the executive vice president for confirmation, the executive vice president remained silent. Of course, this disturbed both mid-level managers.

After the meeting, the executive vice president put his arm around the manager who had attempted to defend his colleague and said, "You must remember, we have a new president—a new pharaoh is in the land. The things that went on before are no longer valid."

When the junior executive protested, "At least you could have verified the truth of the matter," the executive vice president simply patted the junior manager on the shoulder, and restated, "There's a new pharaoh in the land," and walked away. After all, the executive vice president knew that the manager under attack was unpopular with the new president, and to have defended him or to have admitted that he himself had "made a foolish decision" in such a tense situation would only diminish his own standing in the eyes of the new president.

Would you say that the executive vice president was honest? Loyal? How were his priorities of principles ranked?

Once when I was working as a consultant with a large firm, occasionally I sat in on informal daily "coffee-break" sessions with the company's top executives. The company's chairman seemed, in my mind, to fit the mold of an authoritarian. One day the company's communication problems became the topic of discussion. After the session broke up, I was cornered by one of the key executives, who had been with the company for thirty years and had survived all the comings and goings of people. He was among the executives held in the highest regard by the boss. He asked, "How would you evaluate the openness of the communication of this group?" After he had listened to my candid response—that communication was much less than open—he volunteered, with a twinge of confession, "Yes, I have been sitting around this table for over twenty years. Everybody sits on their own ideas until they learn what the boss has on his mind, and then you have never seen such enthusiastic outspokenness supporting the chief's ideas."

In most organizations, when the principles of loyalty and honesty come into conflict, loyalty is the most prudent path to survival.

■ HANDLING CONFLICTS OF PRINCIPLES

People with any degree of sensitivity have experienced conflicts of principles. But what is the best way to deal with them? Although there are no simple solutions, persons of integrity will follow steps similar to the following:

- **1. Recognize that one or more right principles can and do conflict with each other in ways that force the violation of a right principle.** Some people cling to the idea that you can always abide by right principles. Just recognizing the idea that sometimes a right principle, such as honesty or loyalty, must be violated is a healthy step on the path to integrity. To deny that a conflict exists when it does exist, is probably one of the worst deceptions of all.

- **2. Identify the conflicting principles** (e.g., loyalty vs. honesty, or truth vs. kindness, or family time vs. career success). State the conflicts and the consequences of each option clearly.

- **3. Have an established hierarchy of values.** If I lived with my family in an area of dire poverty, would I steal if that were the only way to feed my family? Yes. Not because stealing is right, but because I would regard sustaining my family as a higher value. Would I kill another person to obtain food for my family? No. Avoiding killing is a higher law than feeding my family.

- **4. Select the higher principle from those in conflict.** Persons of integrity "never let things that matter most be at the mercy of things which matter least." When challenged that you violated a right principle, acknowledge that you did, and the reason for doing so was to abide by a higher value.

- **5. Do not get upset if you find that someone has been dishonest to maintain loyalty.** Even "honest" people indulge occasionally in dishonesty to avoid being disloyal to friends.

- **6. Be willing to accept what may appear to be acts of disloyalty.** You must give greater rewards for honesty than for loyalty when they conflict if you truly want to establish honesty as your high-priority principle.

Nearly everyone and every institution believes in the same set of values. What distinguishes one from another is the priority or ranking they give to these common values. Persons of integrity not only struggle choosing between right and wrong, but wrestle mightily selecting the higher of two rights. Enjoy wrestling and the resultant moral strength that comes from engaging in a worthy wrestle for integrity.

CASE: BIRTHDAY SHIRT

Pam and Hal had not been married very long. Pam was so in love with Hal that she wanted to do something extra special for his upcoming birthday. The two were still students, and money was tight. Although she'd had very little experience in sewing, she decided that with time and concentration, she could make a shirt for him, and the effort would show him how much she really cared. For six weeks she worked on the shirt secretly so it would be a total surprise. She completed it just in time for his birthday.

Pam prepared a special dinner and had the meal all ready and the table set by the time Hal arrived home from his part-time job. After they ate dinner, Pam went to the bedroom and retrieved a handsomely wrapped box. Returning to the dinner table, she smiled, gave Hal a tender kiss and a hug, and wished him a happy birthday.

Hal carefully removed the paper and opened the box while Pam watched with heightened anticipation. The style of collar and pattern of cloth left Hal feeling that he would not want to be seen in public wearing the shirt. He had never worn a color like that nor would he want to. And when he held it up, he could tell right away that the sleeves would not fit.

At that moment, Pam leaned forward and with excitement in her voice asked, "How do you like the shirt, dear? I made it myself."

QUESTIONS

1. If you were Hal, what would you say next?

2. Is this a time to be perfectly honest? Does this situation justify lying?

3. Keep in mind that "I really appreciate the effort you put into making it" really doesn't cut it, because Pam asked how Hal liked the shirt. So, if you were Hal and Pam prodded you for your answer, how would respond to her now?

4. If you were Pam, how would you want Hal to respond?

CREATE A CLIMATE
WHERE WRONGFUL
ACTS CAN BE REPORTED

CHAPTER NINE

The Perils of Whistle-Blowing

SHORTLY AFTER the Challenger space shuttle disaster, I was teaching a business ethics class at the University of Utah. I had heard that a nationally known company that supplied equipment and materials to the U.S. Department of Defense had introduced a new program on ethical behavior. Since I knew the person who had started the new program, I invited him to speak to my class to explain how the program worked and what results the company was experiencing. I hoped that, in a time when business managers and politicians were being fired upon with accusations of unethical behavior, this lecturer could engender a healthy respect in the minds of my students for the moral integrity of most people in the "real world."

The man explained the details of the company's ethics program and the philosophy behind it. One of the key elements of the program was to encourage employees to behave more honestly by providing incentives for those who report the unethical behavior of others. For example, the company wanted to discourage the dishonest practice of employees punching each other's time cards. Whenever employees knew they would be coming in late or wanted to get away from work early, they could ask fellow workers to punch their time cards at the regular time. By fudging by an hour or so, they could still receive a full paycheck. Reciprocity in this practice was common, and over time, this practice generated a system of mutual obligation.

The company expected that by rewarding those who reported such practices, which also included receiving gifts or favors from suppliers or taking bogus sick days, it could stop or minimize them and create a climate of a higher standard of moral behavior. However, he explained, the training was just underway and it was hard to tell how it was working.

In his discussion with the students he was asked, "So I guess you must be recruiting that engineer from Thiokol?" The student was referring to an engineer with Morton Thiokol who, during the investigation after the Challenger disaster, explained that he had warned Thiokol's management that the shuttle's O-rings could fail in low temperatures, but that his supervisors had ignored his warnings and told him to keep quiet. After the engineer had been candid and honest in reporting the experience to investigators, management tried to fire him.

The student felt that this man would certainly fit in with the lecturer's company since it employed many engineers in the defense industry, and he seemed to fit with the company philosophy of reporting wrongdoing. But, the students were surprised by my friend's reply to the suggestion, "No! We wouldn't hire him. That engineer went about reporting the incident in the wrong way."

■ BUCKING THE SYSTEM

The new ethics program my friend's company was trying to implement had at least two flaws: First, the program was bucking against human nature and the deeply ingrained value our culture instills in us at a very young age and reinforces throughout our lives: "Don't be a tattletale!"

Over the years I have tried to find out whether people were hesitant to point out wrongdoing simply because the consequences for the person reported were minor or petty. I reasoned that maybe people felt they were being nice by not inflicting their associates with compliance to burdensome

In many instances, the government also has difficulty enticing people to report illegal practices. For example, the Utah state government gets frustrated by people who license their vehicles in other states, but then drive them illegally in Utah. Utah law requires that after you have taken up residence in the state, you have ninety days to register your car and obtain Utah license plates. But some drivers license their cars in Oregon, for instance, because the registration costs less than in Utah. Then, by using a former address or by claiming a parent's home in Oregon as their address, they continue to retain Oregon licenses and registrations even though they live in Utah and are not students or temporary residents.

Finding that many vehicle owners engaged in this practice, one Utah sheriff appealed to the members of his community to report suspected violations in their neighborhoods or places of work. He asked people to report vehicles with out-of-state license plates that parked in their neighborhoods over extended periods of time, such as two years. He promised that they could retain complete anonymity—if they would just give the location, description, and license

(continued on next page)

regulations, or perhaps they felt hypocritical by reporting someone else's misdeeds when they, themselves, wouldn't obey such rules. But I find that even when someone has committed a gross criminal act, people are still extremely hesitant to report it. The dilemma is simply another example of conflict of principle: wanting to be loyal versus wanting to correct wrongdoing. For most people, loyalty wins out—even in cases of gross misbehavior.

This is more than just struggling against the noble value of loyalty; you are dealing with a basic cultural value—"don't snitch," "don't squeal," "don't be a stool pidgin," "don't be a tattletale."

However, even though whistle-blowing occurs infrequently, and with unusual agony, it does occur. The case of the "Unabomber" is an interesting example. For eighteen years someone had been regularly sending deadly bombs through the mail. The anonymous mail bombs had caused the deaths of three people and had injured twenty-three others. For years, authorities had tracked every lead to no avail. In the early part of 1996, the published reports of the bombings began to catch the interest of David Kaczymnski, who picked up a few of the clues and began to suspect his brother, Theodore Kaczymnski. After a lengthy analysis of his own, he became convinced that his brother was the Unabomber, and he reported Theodore to the authorities. An FBI agent investigating the case commented, "He [David] was as torn as anyone would be between doing what is socially right and loyalty to his brother."[1] As heinous as the crime was, it took considerable internal debate and agonizing for David to come forward and "do the right thing."

David didn't see himself as a hero—far from it. In fact, he became angry when news leaked to the press that he had "squealed" on his brother. Many people empathized with his difficulty and asked themselves, "Would I turn someone in?"

number, the sheriff's deputies would handle the rest. He gave several good, rational arguments for the local citizens to report the cars: Their tax dollars were subsidizing these "scroungers" who refuse to pay their fair share to keep up state roads and provide for police protection; they would not have to pay any social price because no one would know who reported the cars, and they could take pride and satisfaction in helping to secure law and order in the community. But, even with all the logical arguments, very few people in the community volunteered to help the sheriff by anonymously blowing the whistle on their neighbors.

The deeply ingrained cultural commandment, "Don't be a tattletale," creates such an environment of guilt for going against it that even logic and rational thinking cannot surmount it. At the time of the Utah license plate problem, I asked the forty students in my university class, "How many of you would help the sheriff if you knew a vehicle in your neighborhood was in violation of the law?" Hesitantly, one hand went up. I have found similar results in discussing other cases of whistle-blowing.

especially if the person was a family member. Many were grateful for David's action, but found it difficult to call him a hero.

■ SELF-POLICING

For the same reason, it is difficult, if not impossible, for most organizations, professional societies, trade associations, churches, and governments to police themselves, despite that many associations and organizations may strongly argue that they *do* police their own members effectively. They often feel it is just a matter of instilling individual integrity in its members, and in some matters they are successful. However, people who really understand integrity realize that personal commitment is not the only element of the formula. The other element, subjection to pressure from other obligations, creates the conflict of choosing between two goods. For instance, which should one choose, to be loyal to your shareholders in keeping stock value high or to report inappropriate conduct?

Once when I was serving on a university athletic committee, a competing university was caught violating NCAA regulations and was suspended from play. In our next committee meeting, the discussion centered on finding out if our university was guilty of similar behavior. We also wondered how the rival university had been caught. One of the coaches gave an interesting insight: He said the NCAA has no police to enforce the rules. The only way the association can find an occasional violator is if a rival school files a report. So, he explained, the reason violations seldom surface is "because we are all doing something that is not appropriate, so we feel hypocritical about reporting someone else." Such a system makes self-policing difficult, if not impossible.

Similar difficulties in reporting are found in the medical profession. Most doctors hate the idea of serving as witnesses against a fellow professional, especially one they know on a personal basis. If you add to that the threat that the accused person might file a lawsuit against a witness or accuser for slander, libel, or character assassination, then only the most grossly unethical conduct will ever get reported.

■ WHISTLE-BLOWING CAN BE DANGEROUS

Intuitively, you would think that in a society that preaches morality and with leaders who "insist" on high standards of ethical integrity, the people who point out corrupt conduct would be held up as heroes and role models, or that companies would reward such people as the epitome of loyalty. But reporting wrongdoings is not just a social no-no; it can be dangerous to your career and possibly even your life.

For example, an April 1996 evening news report announced that two airplane mechanics testified in a Senate subcommittee investigative hearing about unethical inspection practices and safety violations in the airline industry. The mechanics, along with the senators who were questioning them, felt that because their testimony would be incriminating to airline companies, their lives would be in danger. So, to reduce the potential threat, their names were withheld from the public, their faces were shielded from the cameras, and their voices were disguised. This incident further demonstrates the depth of our cultural bias against whistle-blowers.

Although many organizations, especially police forces, go to great lengths to protect whistle-blowers, it is still difficult, in fact almost impossible, to keep back the forces that oppose them—just ask anyone who has blown a whistle. Besides requiring courage, whistle-blowers, with few exceptions, must be willing to pay a social and/or economic price. Even managers who admire whistle-blowers for their courage in exposing fraud, or cheating, or embezzlement in other organizations would hesitate to hire such people into their own organizations because they question the loyalty of such people.

■ **WHEN TRUSTED LIEUTENANTS BLOW THE WHISTLE**

A letter to the editor of *Chief Financial Officers* magazine describes one such case in which a chief financial officer, Mr. Nazeley, didn't even blow the whistle—he just took exception to the company's president. Imagine what might have happened if he had chosen to go public with his problem.

No one really can discuss ethics unless he has been asked to do something that is unethical. Ethics has a different meaning to each of us. *And I have never met anyone who didn't believe that he or she had high morals before an ethical issue forced a certain decision.*

Faced with such a dilemma, you must weigh loyalty to family against loss of employment and income. You must also deal with the frustration and stress of the situation, as well as eventually facing the day of the dreaded decision.

Being a CFO does not spare you this anguish. CFOs have to care for the needs of themselves, their families, their employers and professional responsibilities just like everyone else. This is a very stressful situation and a constant balancing act.

What compounds everything is that we live in a world of financial survival. Without money, no one can exist. . . . Everyone has financial problems. If you quit, you could be out of work for years. The employer will not give you a favorable reference, and who is going to hire a CFO without references? You could tell a prospective employer your dilemma, but most people don't want to hire problems. If you quit without a reason, you will not collect unemployment, the employer knows you quit for a reason and generally will not give you a good reference. Your friends will tell you to sue for breach of employment ethics and hope you get a settlement. But what lawyer will take this case on contingency?

Once you have been through this type of ethical dilemma, you become more understanding of the motivating factors. I am a white knight who did the right thing and was out of work for eighteen months, losing my self-respect in the process. Was it worth it? That is a personal question that I don't have the answer to. But please, God, don't offer me this choice again [emphasis added.][2]

If resigning in such an instance could cause such a cost, imagine the price he and his family would have paid if he had chosen to blow the whistle and expose the unethical behavior.

In another letter to the editor in the same magazine, the writer requested that his or her name be withheld even though he/she had already been tried and was serving a jail sentence.

After reading, "A Question of Ethics," it seemed as if you had published my story. I was CFO of a company in Savannah, Georgia, during 1989. Everything was going fine until the owner decided to expand and, in the process, hire people under the Federal Job Training Partnership Act (JTPA).

At the beginning, it seemed that through the JTPA the company would be helping people train for good jobs. But as the program progressed and the City of Savannah began to pay the fees for training new employees, I noticed that the workers were never available when I tried to check on their progress and personally supervise the program. I should add, however, that when it came time for these people to sign their time sheets, they were always present.

After several months, telephone calls from the JTPA office started coming in, and the owner was the only one allowed to field them. My instincts told me that something was very wrong, and when I started asking questions, I found out that the owner was not paying the JTPA employees as he was supposed to. Instead, he was keeping the money for his personal use.

My response to this information was to quit, and for nearly two years I had no contact with my ex-employer. Then, one day a Labor Department investigator showed up at my house asking about my employment. In time, there was court action, and I had to relay what I knew of the JTPA incident and my reasons for quitting. But that was not enough. According to the government officials, I should have reported the suspected problems to the JTPA office. *I was charged with conspiracy to commit fraud.*

Right now, I have five months to serve, five months of home confinement, and three years probation for not knowing what the owner was doing. The sentence is not the worst part. My career has been destroyed because I tried to do the job I was being paid to do. I learned the hard way that a CFO has no witnesses or friends, and that owners will not back you up when things go wrong. The way I see it, there is more risk working at the top of management than at the bottom of the ladder [emphasis added].[3]

If whistle-blowing is required by law (and it appears that it is), it can place people in impossible circumstances. If they speak out, they become social outcasts and are suspected of disloyalty, but if they don't their consciences—and possibly the law—will take their toll. Such people will pay a very high price regardless of whether they blow the whistle or not.

In another letter, the person also asked that the magazine withhold his or her name, even though the writer doesn't identify any wrongdoing. Apparently, just discussing the possibility of blowing the whistle was so threatening that the person didn't want to be identified. Perhaps the person worried that if his or her employer learned of these feelings, the person would be suspected of disloyalty.

Professor Leo V. Ryan [referring to the article's author] writes that integrity is the most important quality of a CFO. But the truth is that loyalty and allegiance to the business owner of a closely held company are what's essential.

Management positions, particularly in the areas of accounting and finance, require walking the fine line between right and wrong as well as crossing that line when the owners demand it. My responsibility as a CFO is to inform owners of the consequences of that action, then move forward, realizing I am placing myself in a tenuous position at the same time.

Ethics, personal and professional, are important to me. And there may be a time when I, in good conscience, cannot cross that line. If that time comes, I will properly advise the owners and pray that they take my advice. If they won't I will resign.[4]

Other than the fact that this person's name was withheld, two other aspects about this letter are interesting: (1) Apparently, on one or more occasions, this person had already crossed the ethical line "in good conscience," but felt that if the time came when crossing the line would violate conscience then he or she would resign. (It's curious: What would allow this person to be unethical "in good conscience" in one instance and not in another? Is it a matter of degree of how much such an action might cost? Is it whether or not "everyone is doing it?")   (2) This person explains that, if asked to do something that would force him or her to cross the line and not "in good conscience," the person would definitely resign, but blowing the whistle isn't even an alternative. This suggests the person's acute awareness of the devastating effects of whistle-blowing.

■ WHEN WHISTLE-BLOWING IS SOCIALLY ACCEPTABLE

In some areas, whistle-blowing seems to have gained some acceptance. For example, cellular phone owners on the highways of large cities are often encouraged to report suspected drunk drivers by calling 911. Law enforcement officials have been receiving many useful tips from cellular owners who are helping to curb the problem. What about this arrangement gives people the impetus to violate the "don't be a tattletale" rule, and how can we apply this example to other cases in which we need more willing whistle-blowers?

- **The targeted behavior is widely accepted as wrong.** Drunk driving, with its gruesome tales of traffic accidents, personal tragedies, and family and community suffering, is almost universally condemned. Messages are widely publicized for people to designate drivers, call taxis, and to not let friends drive drunk. It seems that only defense attorneys are willing to stick up for drunk drivers these days. Drinking and driving has no redeeming virtue. There is little or no conflicting value to counter its widely accepted wrongness.

- **People understand how the wrong behavior directly affects them.** Most sober drivers can see how a drunk driver could affect them here and now. Also, many people are personally acquainted with families who have been devastated by drunk drivers, or even by alcoholism alone.

- **Reporting illegal behavior will lead immediately to positive results.** Reporting a suspected drunk driver will direct a police officer to the scene within minutes and, hopefully, get the drunk driver off the road before any physical harm is done.

- **Fourth, it's simple and anonymous.** With a phone at the ready and many cellular phones on the highway, callers can be confident that no one will ever find out who reported the incident.

- **Reporting total strangers seems easier than reporting a friend or boss.** It's more like filing a report than "tattling" on a person, reporting an event instead of confronting someone. It always seems easier to take action against a "thing" than a person you know.

Applying these five characteristics to other cases where we need more willing whistle-blowers would help us reduce the social pressure on whistle-blowing.

TAKING ACTION

What should a corporation do?

1) *Discuss the impact of unchecked unethical behavior in the workplace* and the impact of a whistle-blowing culture. Be prepared to deal with the fallout of the discussion if you are in a "don't ask, don't tell" environment. Talk, talk, talk, not in preachy generalities, but use specific incidents like the Ronald MacNeil case at the end of this chapter, the CFOs' experiences, and incidents from your own organization.

2) *Determine if establishing a culture of whistle-blowing will help your situation* and discuss the idea with your group. Educate your group about the need for such a culture and discuss the pros and cons of how a whistle-blowing program would affect the group and the individuals in it. Make a group decision to work together on the plan that will work best.

(continued on page 120)

(continued from page 119)

3) Identify the specific steps that are needed to establish whistle-blowing as a socially acceptable part of your group's culture. A single memo will not change a culture. Instead, plan a sustained effort to implement the program and get feedback from participants. Use the feedback to improve or change the program.

4) Select only one or two aspects of your group's activities to work on in the beginning. Do not try to encourage everyone to report every kind of suspected behavior at once.

5) Be prepared to become the target of whistle-blowers if you are a leader and want to develop a culture that permits or encourages whistle-blowing, Sadly, sometimes the value of exposing wrongdoing is neutralized by accusations made out of vengeance. Be courageous and recognize that some of that may just be the price of validly exposing wrongdoing.

After reading the general guidelines above, the actual experience of one organization, we will call the XYZ Company, may help stimulate specific ideas.

Thirteen years ago the XYZ Company decided to establish an "Anonymous Reporting" program to expose and correct unethical behavior among its employees. Paul Hill was appointed vice president and ethics officer. He arranged for a special phone on his desk with a specific number for anonymous calls. The program and the guidelines were announced over the company's communication system with emphasis on "absolute anonymity."

The first two or three years the calls were few and all anonymous. Apparently for many months employees were testing if the management was serious about this program and also to verify if Paul could be trusted. Every accusation was investigated—falsifying time cards, stealing, harrassment, violations of gift policy, etc.—and where appropriate, disciplinary action was taken.

The accused often made a significant effort to identify the "reporter" and sometimes even when they couldn't identify who "squealed" on them, they would conclude who they thought it was. These surmises could lead to some strained relationships. The management was very conscious of minimizing the tendency to build a climate of distrust with "Anonymous Reporting."

After about three years, the overall confidence in the program, and Paul, grew to where most of the reports were face-to-face with Paul and the minority were anonymous; that is, few accusers kept their identities from Paul, even though confidentiality kept anyone else from knowing who they were.

The XYZ Company feels the program has been a success. On average, Paul receives just under two complaints a week, or less than one hundred over a year's time in this company of 2,000 employees in four locations. Seventy-one percent of accusations are validated. Twenty-nine percent are found to be false or cannot be validated.

One of the objectives of the program has been to provide a way of handling wrongdoing internally so employees will not feel a need to go public with their whistle-blowing. Paul feels they have been very successful with very few going outside to stockholders or the public with reports of wrongdoing.

Here are seven observations Paul feels have been important to their success:

1 **The ethics officer should be independent from other corporate departments.** He or she should not be in human resources or the legal department because of inevitable conflicts of interest.

2 **The ethics officer must take time for employees to build confidence in him or her personally.** This requires strict keeping of promises and the appearance of keeping promises on the part of the officer.

3 **Absolute confidentiality must be preserved.** No one in the company ever knows the name of an accuser except Paul and his secretary. All names are kept in a locked file. Not even the president of the company is ever given the name of an accuser.

4 **Handling false or unproven accusations with confidentiality is just as important as validated ones.**

5 **There is a strictly enforced policy of no retaliation or attempted retaliation against a reporter or supposed reporter.**

6 **Keep the program in front of all employees.** Promote it regularly through communication channels. XYZ Company uses staff meetings as reminders, as well as Web site and periodic tests of employees' knowledge of company ethical policies generally and "Anonymous Reporting" specifically.

7 **XYZ Company feels that many reports is the evidence the program is working.** Few reports would indicate a poorly functioning program.

At the end of his junior year of high school, Ron MacNeil was looking around his hometown for a summer job. After about a week, he heard that an electrical supply warehouse was moving to another town nearly thirty miles away and was looking for temporary help to accomplish the move. Ron applied and was hired at minimum wage for the duration of the moving job. He found himself working with four other young men, three of whom he already knew fairly well. The five estimated that the job would probably last about three weeks.

The boys worked well together and did their jobs to the satisfaction of their employer. They kept careful count of their hours worked, but they were surprised when their first week's pay was noticeably less than what they had expected. When they brought the matter to their employer's attention, he blandly informed them that they could hardly expect to be paid for the time they spent riding in the truck from one town to the other. He also reminded them that summer employment was not easy for high school students to find that year.

Ron and the others were furious, and they were convinced that the owner was cheating them. Next week, the other four boys started slipping wire, switches, and other supplies into their pockets and urged Ron to do the same. Although he agreed that they had been treated unfairly, Ron refused to join them in pilfering supplies and threatened to report them if they continued the practice. When they threatened to "get him" if he gave them away, Ron decided to remain silent, though he still did not participate in taking supplies.

QUESTIONS

1. Was the employer justified in refusing to pay for travel time?

2. If not, were the boys right in making up their wages by taking supplies?

3. If they were not, was Ronald justified in keeping silent about the matter?

4. Were you in Ronald's position, what would you do?

5. If you were an employer trying to prevent a situation like this, what would you do?

CHAPTER TEN

None Dare Call It Bribery:
The Law of Obligation

PEOPLE OFTEN THINK of bribery as one of those problems primarily associated with businesses that operate in foreign countries. But the problem is large scale right here in "River City, USA." Most people are just reluctant to call it "bribery."

A man I will call Harper Kellog, an executive of a very large corporation, was responsible for deciding who should receive the large contracts his organization lets out at regular intervals. They vary in size from a few thousand dollars to $5 million. Usually the amount is somewhere between $100,000 and $1 million. Kellog was answering questions after a lecture to an MBA marketing class when the following exchange took place:

"Mr. Kellog," one student asked, "I am interested to know, if I were representing a company that was bidding for a contract from your organization, what could I do to influence your decision? Is your decision based solely on cost?"

"Cost is always a major factor in contract-letting in our business," he replied. "But you must keep in mind that in this business the product and service we are looking for is complicated and often one-of-a-kind, so we also must make significant judgments about many intangibles like a contractor's reliability, the competence of management and engineering staff, financial stability, and other factors."

"Then," continued the student, "could an effective sales representative make a difference in a decision?"

"Well yes, but only so far as he is able to give us evidence of the contractor's capacity with regard to the intangibles I just mentioned," responded Kellog.

Another student asked, "Mr. Kellog, I am aware that one of your contractors keeps a hunting and fishing lodge in Minnesota where the company regularly entertains potential clients. Is this kind of entertaining an effective tool to influence contract decisions?"

"No, I can honestly say it is not," Kellog responded quickly and assertively. "We must make judgments based on the facts. On one occasion the contractor you refer to took my wife and me to the lodge for a ten-day hunting vacation, and we had a marvelous time. But I can honestly say that the trip had absolutely no influence on any decisions I have to make when choosing contractors."

National politicians make similar statements, admitting that they receive significant favors from certain business and labor interests, while at the same time maintaining that the favors have no influence on their decisions or positions.

While some executives make defensive statements like this, knowing that they are not being honest, others make similar statements and honestly think that what they are saying is so. Beware of both groups: People in the first group are not to be trusted, and those in the second group have questionable competence, for they are naive if not just plain ignorant about the nature of obligation. This ignorance and the assertions resulting from it contribute greatly to the public's distrust and skepticism of all executives' and politicians' public declarations and their overall credibility.

Understanding the subtle nature of obligation would help businesspeople, especially those who have been trapped in its web to 1) avoid stepping unwittingly into compromising situations and 2) shun statements about gifts (and everything else) that are patently unbelievable, and thereby prevent further damage to their credibility problem.

No one can accept a favor or gift of kindness, no matter how small, from another person without incurring an obligation. Or, to state it another way, every time we accept a favor or gift from another person, we incur an obligation. This is the law of obligation.

We can better understand and clarify it by considering three questions: 1) What is an obligation? 2) How are obligations incurred, and how do they arise? and 3) Is it wrong to incur obligations?

An obligation, according to the dictionary, is "any duty imposed by law, promise or contract, moral or social ties, etc."[1] The last part of this definition, "social ties," can have great significance for business executives. The definition of *duty* which is a synonym for *obligation* may help highlight the implications of obligations. *Duty* means: "That which a person is *bound to do,* as a responsible person; the compulsion felt to meet such obligation" [emphasis added].[2]

Most normal people instinctively and subconsciously sense that they are "bound to do" something when they receive a gift or favor, even though they may feel uncomfortable about it. Nevertheless, even though a duty or obligation may cause discomfort or risk, any responsible person is, by definition, bound to do that which is expected by the obligation, as long as the expectation is proportionate to the degree of obligation.

Rolf Mengele, son of the infamous Dr. Josef Mengele who caused the deaths of thousands of people in the German concentration camps of World War II, couldn't bring himself to report his father to the authorities during the years of search following the war. In 1985, the year Dr. Mengele's bones were discovered (six years after his death in Brazil), Rolf was asked why he had never turned his father in. He explained that he couldn't turn in his father. Then, even after his father had died, Rolf kept the information to himself because he felt an obligation to protect those who had sheltered his father.[3] Obligations can bind people in ways that cause them to act unethically.

The law of obligation can be very simple and subtle, but it is still real. For example, when you go to another person's home and allow the host or hostess to hang your coat in the closet, this simple act obligates you to stay longer than if you had kept your coat on or held it in your lap. You have to stay long enough to justify the effort and to complete

BIG FAVOR, BIG OBLIGATION

The North Carolina Council of Churches wrestled mightily with the law of obligation when it was about to publish a study on the moral conflicts of tobacco. One of the ministers explained, "We insist there's a moral problem when you're producing a product that causes death to a large number of people." Yet the report began to cause a great deal of anxiety even before it was published. Although council members felt a strong urgency to take a moral stand about the harmful effects of tobacco, the council's long-established obligations to companies in the tobacco industry made the situation difficult and complex, even perilous:

"It would be pretty difficult for a local church pastor to go on a crusade against tobacco when there are large numbers of people in his congregation whose livelihoods depend
(continued on next page)

to go to that much bother. If you leave too early, the host or hostess has the right to feel, "Well, if that's all the time you were going to stay, then why did you allow me to put your coat away?"

Accepting favors or gifts does, indeed, incur an obligation. An oft-repeated childhood maxim conditions us to honor those obligations: "Don't bite the hand that feeds you."

One of the interesting things about obligations is that generally when a duty is first contracted, both parties understand what specific or general thing the other party is bound to do. Also, the size of the originating favor determines the size of obligation incurred. For example, if a legislator accepts a large donation or favor from a labor organization when relevant legislation is pending, the politician is obligated to take a position that could be completely opposite to what his or her position would have been had the favor been accepted from, say a business management group. A small favor would only require the lawmaker to speak for the proposition, but a large favor would require significant campaigning and arm twisting for the organization's cause on the part of the legislator, along with his guaranteed vote.

on it," says Dennis Campbell, dean of Duke University's Divinity School.

When one committee member is asked if he would raise the morality issue in his church, he says, "I'm not sure I dare." And with good reason: "If a preacher were to start something, he wouldn't be here long. We'd ship him out," says Gil Richardson. . . .[4]

But how did the obligation get to be so strong that it could bind these ministers so they couldn't speak out on issues of life and death? Simple: Over the years they had accepted great gifts and favors. For example, Duke University was called Trinity College until 1924, when it was given $6 million by James B. Duke, a tobacco magnate. The Duke Endowment (founded with tobacco money) continues to provide funds for rural Methodist churches and a small pension to all retired Methodist ministers in North Carolina.

While in many situations the obligation is mutually understood, there are other times just what is expected is not clear at the time the "social tie" or obligation occurs. Frequently, when a person accepts a gift or favor, it is left open as to when the corresponding duty will be fulfilled and exactly what might be required, like a blank check. The undated, undesignated check is placed in the drawer for some future need and isn't cashed in until the person granting the gift or favor has needs or desires arising that would merit it. The obligation may range from a simple introduction to a helpful contact or the sharing of useful information, all the way up to providing major support for a desired cause. This kind of open-ended obligation, without knowing at the time what form of payment could be requested, is the most dangerous of obligations. It often entraps the unwitting and binds them to do things that they otherwise would not do.

For our purposes here, an obligation is "that which a person is bound to do because of social ties." Innate in almost everyone is the feeling that we can't turn our backs on people who have done us a favor or who have been of help. When someone requests our assistance, we are generally inwardly compelled, because of some past gift or favor, to respond with help, even if we never asked for the original favor but it was given voluntarily. We often hear businesspeople, particularly executives say, "He owes me one," when they are trying to decide whom they should ask for help. Likewise, whenever an organization is seeking the cooperation or contribution of some other person or company, the "right" person is sent to make the request. That person is often the one to whom the "debtor" is socially bound or obligated because of past favors or gifts. It would be difficult to turn down the "collector" without an extremely good reason.

HOW ARE OBLIGATIONS INCURRED, AND HOW DO THEY ARISE?

How, then, are obligations incurred? How do the circumstances arise?

One of the most subtle obligations arises when a "receiver" asks for no favor, but is given something voluntarily. For instance, suppose a piece of property is coming up for sale adjacent to a receiver's property, which he would like very much to own. But, before he or the public can learn about it, an "obligator" or "giver" learns of it and says, "Say, I just heard that land next door to you is coming up for sale. An announcement will be made in about a week. If you want to do something before then, I suggest you contract Mike Riggs. He's handling it. If you don't know him, I'll be happy to introduce you—just thought you'd like to know."

If the man acts on this information, he automatically incurs an obligation. If he agrees to be introduced, a greater obligation is incurred. Even if he does not act on the tip, he also may incur a slight obligation just because the giver offered to be helpful.

Some may protest, "No way—nothing happened," and try to show that the two had no agreement, so no one is obligated to do anything. But such a response either is self-deceiving or comes from ignorance or naivete about social relations. Remember, any accepted favor incurs an obligation.

The story of the godfather is the principle of obligations at work in its clearest form: The godfather sees a man who does not have the money to pay for a proper burial for his wife, so he steps forward and offers the man money to cover the funeral costs.

"No," says the man, "I can't accept your offer because I could not repay it."

"Don't worry," says the godfather. "I just want to do something nice for you. It's a gift."

Later, when the godfather returns and asks for a favor that seems highly suspect and unethical, the man realizes that he is bound to a contract made some time ago without even realizing it. But it is now difficult or impossible to turn his back on the request.[5]

Consider what happens when a salesman calls your home and says, "Your name has been selected by our company to receive a free gift. May I deliver it to your home tomorrow night? There is no obligation."

You say, "Yes, I guess that would be okay."

The following night he rings the doorbell and says, "Here is your gift," and hands you a small calculator or a deluxe pen set. "Would you mind signing this form to indicate that I delivered your gift?" While you are signing the paper, he continues, "By the way, our company has just come out with a new life insurance policy. Could I take just a few minutes of your time to explain how valuable it could be for you?"

Do you have any obligation to let him in for "a few minutes?" Surely after the salesman has gone to all that bother and has driven all that way to deliver your "free gifts," he reasons, you will listen to him for at least five to ten minutes. Now, you are not obligated to buy, because that would mean a repayment larger than the obligation, but only the most crass would flatly turn away the salesman without at least some twinge of conscience.

But when did you incur the obligation? When did you "sign the contract?" It happened when you said, "Yes, I guess that would be okay."

In fact, the insurance company is fully aware of the psychological obligation and has deliberately designed its sales approach to take advantage of that principle. When the salesman told you there was no obligation, it was a lie. He conveyed a false impression if he did not, at least, expect you to listen to his pitch.

When a person *asks* for a gift or favor from another person and the person grants it, the obligation is more binding and usually requires a greater return on demand than if the favor had been volunteered.

Suppose an executive has ambitions of becoming the president of a business organization. He approaches the president of the local chamber of commerce, knowing that the president has a strong influence with the chairman of the organization's selection committee. He tells him that he would like to become president of the organization and asks, "Would you mind putting in a good word for me?" The president obliges and makes a considerable effort to influence the board on behalf of the executive. Later, when the chamber president comes around to ask the new president to purchase supplies from one of his own companies or a friend's company the president may be obligated to purchase from that company even if another supplier has a better offer.

In attempting to avoid the negative effects of obligations, some companies establish what may seem to be rather rigid policies. One company does not allow any of its employees to go to lunch with suppliers or potential suppliers unless the employees pay for their own meals. Ten-day hunting excursions, weekend entertainment packages, and basketball tickets are definitely out. Any supplier maintaining an entertainment account would be suspect of attempting to incur obligations.

Although we must exercise great caution when making generalized statements, we must nonetheless admit that no area of human interaction—professional, religious, private, or otherwise—is free from challenges created by the law of obligation. Here are a few examples of how the law of obligation affects certain industries:

Medicine. One day I attended a seminar meeting with the staff of a medical school and the representatives of a large pharmaceutical company. The meeting was conducted by a medical doctor who was designated as the medical school's "ethicist." The discussion centered around the free dinners sponsored once a week for the hospital's resident interns by the pharmaceutical company: Once a week, all of the interning doctors were expected to review their experiences at a meeting with the medical staff. The meetings were generally held in conjunction with a dinner sponsored by the pharmaceutical company, which seemed to work much better for the residents than if no dinner was served. In fact, when the meetings were held without dinners, attendance dropped significantly, so the hospital invited the company to keep sponsoring the meals.

However, other pharmaceutical companies began to voice concerns that the dinners gave the sponsoring company an unfair advantage. For example, residents at the dinners were reminded of the company's generosity in sponsoring the meal, and at each meal the company had the opportunity to introduce one or two new products. The pharmaceutical company reasoned that the expense was justified because, by associating this act of generosity with the company's products during the residents' formative professional years, the residents would be enthusiastic about recommending or prescribing company products to patients in their individual practices. On the other hand, the medical school and hospital had no budget money allocated for the dinners, and the company had provided a helpful boost to the school in improving the learning process.

Some faculty members questioned the ethics of the practice. They felt that the dinners incurred some very real obligations that might or might not be in the best interest of future patients. Also, the practice seemed to be incurring certain obligations for the medical school. Still, the faculty felt that resident attendance at the dinner meetings was very important, and many residents, faculty members, and businesses saw nothing wrong with the practice. They argued, as do many people who engage in such practices, that the school's and students' professional judgments would not be swayed by accepting such favors.

During the same discussion, the doctors and the pharmaceutical company representatives discussed the practice of pharmaceutical salespeople providing doctors with free samples of new products. Did such a practice incur questionable obligations for the doctors? A company representative volunteered, "We would love to get rid of the practice of providing free samples."

One of the doctors asked, "Well, then why do you keep doing it?"

"Every time we limit or cut off free samples our sales drop significantly. We can't afford to stop the practice," he replied.

During the discussion, I recalled that I had recently gone to see my doctor for a checkup. He was a young, new physician, and had not been practicing very long. He asked me, "Are you taking any medications?"

"Occasionally I take [a brand-name, over-the-counter antacid] that my former doctor recommended for upset stomach," I replied.

"Well," he said, "we don't know yet, but there may be some negative side effects with that medication." He opened a cabinet that displayed an ample supply of prescription medication. He handed me a small supply of "free" capsules and said, "Here, take these, and I'll write you a prescription so you can have a supply on hand."

I followed his instructions because I have confidence in the medical profession. But, when I went to get the prescription filled, I found that the new drug cost many times more than what I had been using. Since then I reflected that I can never remember a doctor recommending an over-the-counter alternative nor suggest that I might ask the pharmacist if there is a less expensive generic brand. Some doctors may do such a thing, but I have not experienced such help in healing the stress on my pocketbook. On the other hand, knowing the law of obligation it is very easy to understand how the convenience of the free samples and a desire to respond to the generosity of the drug company can subtly combine to produce that specific prescription.

Later on in the same meeting, another doctor volunteered that he and his wife had been invited recently to go to Palm Springs for a three-day seminar sponsored by a drug manufacturer, with all expenses paid by the sponsor. He estimated the total cost of the trip would have been about $5,000. He explained that the three days were filled with vacation activities including golf, sightseeing, fine dinners, and so forth. The only obligation he had was to attend a one-hour "educational session on pharmaceuticals" at some time during the three days. No one in the meeting spoke out saying that was wrong. It seems that they felt it was common practice and acceptable for companies to sponsor such trips. Around the time of the medical ethics meeting, the *New England Journal of Medicine* reported:

> We must recognize that these enticements [gifts, trips, honorariums, etc.] are not entirely free because they add to costs that are passed on to consumers—our patients. As Rawlins noted in 1984, "Few doctors accept that they, themselves, have been corrupted. Most doctors believe that they are quite untouched by the seductive ways of industry's marketing . . . that they can enjoy a company's 'generosity' in the form of gifts and hospitality without prescribing product. The degree to which the profession, mainly composed of honorable and decent people, can practice such self-deceit is quite extraordinary."[6]

However, at a more recent medical ethics seminar I attended, it was very encouraging to hear a doctor raise the issue of free trips. She was quite outspoken as she articulated what she felt were the dangers of this activity to good medical practice. More than one doctor volunteered that they observed how they have seen this affect other doctors negatively, but they themselves were above such influence. So it appears the message is beginning to take hold. There are some who recognize the moral questionability of accepting gifts and their attached obligations and have tried to buck the practice.

"Students get textbooks, almost everyone gets stethoscopes, and I've heard there's even free pizzas the third and fourth year," says Joshua Sharfstein, a first year medical student at Harvard University, who shuns such favors as unethical. Last fall, he organized a drive to return free medical dictionaries and textbooks on cranial nerves emblazoned with the name of the pharmaceutical benefactor . . . "Only about ten percent of the first year students," says Sharfstein, "sent their books back."[7]

Do these practices—free samples, retreats, etc.—influence doctors? Do they influence the quality or expense of the care that patients receive from their doctors? Should the practices be discontinued? Legislated? Moderated?

Politics. The problems with bribery and the law of obligation in politics have had widespread attention in the media. One senator's experience, as described in the *Wall Street Journal*, seems to be replicated over and over again by other elected officials.

According to the article, lobbyists seemed to have targeted the senator's two most pressing concerns: (1) getting reelected and (2) supplementing his income sufficiently to help him keep his children in top schools. The lobbyists employed two main devices to help him resolve those concerns: They contributed substantial campaign funds to him and arranged for speaking engagements around the country with honoraria. One prominent lobbyist remarked, "We don't just want to give money to people. We want to get involved in dialogue. The only way to get a favorable hearing is to deal with [the senator's] problems. To the lobbyist, these favors obligate the senator to at least allow access to him. Surely, by accepting the assistance, the politician has incurred some obligation to the lobbyist's cause.

But the senator's reaction to concerns about his capitalizing on the favors was interesting:

> Boy, I'd have taken money from anybody in that campaign, that was my attitude. . . . Maybe in the first couple of years I would have said that [perhaps there is a better way to finance campaigns], maybe even through the campaign. But now there's probably a sense of realism that comes with one reelection that says—that's the way it is. Bad as though it may seem, it's still better than second place. . . . I don't feel sleazy. . . . Having to ask some people that are lobbying out here, and all that sort of thing for money, that doesn't bother me. . . . I'm really not for sale; I can't be bought.[8]

Bob Dole, former chairman of the Senate Finance Committee, once jokingly remarked, "Some of us are uncomfortable taking honoraria. I am uncomfortable taking campaign contributions. So, I compromised: I decided to take both." Many people seriously question whether politicians either don't understand or simply choose to ignore the implications of the law of obligation.

The practice of influence-peddling and favor-exchanging between politicians and corporations is not likely to change as a time-honored American tradition. After all, it gives many American companies who are good at it an advantage over foreign competition. In 1994, Lord Young, the former British Minister of Trade and Industry, explained, "Without kickbacks, British entrepreneurs would be unable to compete abroad. Some foreign businesses say they have difficulty competing in the U.S. market because of the ability of American firms to gain influence through political contributions."[9]

Food Inspection. Peter Schnuck discussed the wrestle with the law of obligation in the meat packing industry in a *Harper's* magazine article. The USDA, it seems, "feels obliged, like all public agencies, to maintain the myth that all rules are rigidly enforced." Yet within the industry it is commonplace knowledge "that if all meat inspection regulations were enforced to the letter, no meat processor in America would be open for business." The inspector has significant discretion: ". . . he is not expected to enforce every rule, but rather to decide which rules are worth enforcing at all."

In an environment where judgments of significant impact are made, meat inspectors are subject to some subtle influences controlled by the packer, including gifts or favors such as office supplies, freezer coats, and "cumshaw" or a gift of meat. Every day packers throw away hundred of pounds of edible meat for one reason or another. According to old-timers at one plant, "It isn't a good inspector who pays for his Sunday dinner." The unwritten code says, "Don't accept more than your family can use," "Don't solicit meat from the packer," and "Don't let cumshaw influence how you do your job." Apparently, these ground rules form an accepted distinction for the industry between a customary gratuity and bribery. Most packers and inspectors feel that the practice facilitates both the working relationship between inspectors and packers and the production process without any negative effects.

"Sure, I accept bundles of meat to take home for my family," says one inspector, echoing many others. "But that doesn't affect my decisions in the plant one iota, and the packer knows that. The fact of the matter is that if you get on a high horse and refuse to take the bundle, it makes it much more difficult to get the job done."[10]

Journalism. The writers and editors of automotive magazines often serve as advisors and consultants to automakers and frequently accept such freebies as airline tickets, rooms at resort hotels, clocks, briefcases, and the free use of some of the hottest cars on the market. One such writer, formerly with *Car and Driver* magazine, claims his writings are "untainted because of his own integrity," and that of the magazine's editors'. "I'm not afraid to bite the hand that somewhat feeds me," he insists. At the same time, these "buff magazines rake in huge amounts by producing 'special issues' that are magazine-length promotions paid by a single manufacturer. . . . But they look just like regular issues."

"I think it's a scandal," says Stephen Isaacs, a professor at Columbia University's School of Journalism. "How can you believe any word in a publication that allows such practices?" [11]

Financial Planning. "Yes, there are certainly frauds out there," says Robert A. Hewitt, chairman of the International Association of Financial Planners. But, "in spite of some of the sensational headlines, most fraud and abuse is perpetrated not by financial planners, but by frauds posing as financial planners."

So how do these crooked planners accomplish their dire deeds? "Crooks use the same marketing and sales techniques that legitimate financial planning professionals use, which is why they're so camouflaged," says Scott Stapf of North American Securities Administrators Association. "Crooked planners will work through community organizations, unions, and church groups, and will make presentations. Afterwards, they get lists of members and move in with sales pitches. It's a very effective way to set up people, because they trust the planner, and *feel guilty about having gotten the free advice*" [emphasis added].[12]

Real Estate. According to a report in the *Wall Street Journal* the law of obligation in the form of an incentive program can affect the price of a house. In real estate it would seem that the law of obligation is carried so far it could be called bribery.

> Home buyers, beware. In many of the nation's real estate markets there is a price on your head. In New York, home sellers are offering $5,000 bonuses to real estate agents who bring them live buyers. In Phoenix, a real estate firm is pooling $250 from each of forty home sellers for a $10,000 door prize for one of the agents who sells their homes. In Southern California, sellers are offering cars to agents who find buyers willing to pay their asking price."[13]

No, bribery—or in these cases, our euphemism for it, the questionable use of the law of obligation—is not just a problem associated with doing business in foreign countries. It exists right here in the U.S.A., even though many people are reluctant to recognize it for what it is. The practice of bribery by manipulation of the law of obligation is universal.

■ IS IT WRONG TO INCUR OBLIGATIONS?

In the normal course of business and social relationships it is practically impossible to avoid incurring obligations. The question becomes, which obligations should be accepted, and which should be rejected? Managers must become astute enough to avoid contracting obligations unwittingly—such are often the worst kind.

By accepting any favor or gift, you are creating a contract of obligation—a duty to repay. Avoid becoming obligated whenever the payment of an obligation might conceivably come in conflict with your own interests or the interests of those to whom you owe a first or greater obligation. The unaware may find themselves bound to do the will of unsavory people who demand payment contrary to their interests or the interests of their organization. In its ugliest form, this is known as blackmail. In milder cases you may find yourself in a situation that causes some embarrassment to you, your boss, or your organization.

Avoid accepting favors or gifts that might influence you later to claim that you felt no obligation or thought the gift or favor would have no influence on you or your decisions. Such claims are the start of a cover-up to avoid embarrassment and only add lying and deceit to indiscretion. Be willing to recognize, if not openly acknowledge, that every obligation has the power to modify, distort, or even destroy objectivity.

On the other hand, some obligations enable us to bind our work groups and partnerships more closely together for better morale and greater cohesiveness, and create a spirit of loyalty and unity. And certainly gifts and favors are part and parcel of family life and true friendship. Often, an attitude of helpfulness can develop in work groups because of the constant stream of favors given between people working together. In one work group, one woman volunteered to help others with their jobs so often that when she came down with an extended illness, the other members of the team felt they owed it to her to preserve her job by working extra hours, without extra pay, so someone else would not be brought in to replace her.

Further, lasting friendships and true love are based on both partners' mutual adherence to the principle of obligation. Acquaintances ripen into friendships as two people strongly feel the need to live up to the obligations that thoughtful deeds and considerations impose upon them. A bond of trust is the result of favors accepted and repaid over time when neither party has failed to repay or at least recognize and express gratitude for the gestures. The reluctance or failure to live up to such obligations can breed distrust.

Before we begin to work with another supplier, we should make sure that we are not still obligated in some way to previous suppliers. And before we deal with potential new customers, we should immediately find out if they are already obligated to other suppliers for the kind of business we would like to do, and to what extent. This same holds for prospective suppliers and contractors. This awareness allows us to assess exactly whose interests should be first in mind and then respect those commitments to the proper extent.

For example, one insurance company manager encouraged his new recruits to buy a new house with a large monthly mortgage payment. According to him, this served as a daily reminder for the recruits to get out and sell enough insurance to meet their payments at the end of each month. But, if I were a prospective customer to such an agent, I would have good reason to question whether he or she really had my interests at heart or whether the obligation overpowered all my concerns in the effort to get my business and earn the commission.

This principle is so subtle and so real to me that I prefer to do all my shopping at stores where the clerks and managers know me personally, rather than at stores where I am a stranger, because those who know me have a greater obligation to be more forthright with me because of our personal friendship.

Obligations are like fire: When they are misused or get out of control they can warp and destroy, but when appropriately applied in the right human relationships, they can warm and empower.

How do we know when the law of obligation is being misused? That is what the study of ethics is all about. Ethics are applied morality and society's guide to differentiating the appropriate uses of such things from the inappropriate uses. This is why we must improve our awareness and search for definitions that are clear enough to serve as useful guidelines for future behavior.

Some companies have already come up with enforceable policies. Here are a few examples:

- "It is unethical for any employee to accept any gifts, lunches, or tickets for entertainment from anyone who supplies or contracts with the company."
- "It is unethical for employees involved in purchasing or contracting decisions to pursue negotiations with potential suppliers who employ or routinely subcontract to a close relative of the employees. Such negotiations are to be handled by another employee of the company."
- "It is unethical for employees to be involved in making decisions that benefit another company if they have a vested interest in the other company."

■ NONE DARE CALL IT BRIBERY

The trick is deciding where acceptable influence ends and bribery begins. Where is the line—lunch? entertainment? holiday gifts? The dictionary's definition of bribery is this: "money or favor given or promised to a person in a position of trust to influence his or her judgment or conduct—something that serves to induce or influence."[14]

If we take this definition at face value, and if we begin with the premise that bribery is unethical, we soon begin to raise some very serious questions about the morality of many widely used sales practices. After all, most lunches, free trips, tickets to entertainment events, and other gifts are employed basically to *induce or influence* someone's judgment or conduct. If salespeople and purchasers did not influence others in ways that brought the desired results—increased sales or reduced operating

BRIBERY AND PRESSURE OF RESULTS

When the pressure for results gets high enough, even individuals and organizations known for their honorable reputations have been found to engage in acts that are, by definition, bribery. Details of bribery are often kept from the public spotlight, and those involved seem to engage in self-justification by rationalizing, "The action was justified because the results were so very important."

Such was the case when a large regional retailer announced that it would be opening a new store in a city where it had previously had no outlet. Initially the chain's management favored a newly developing area on the edge of the city for the location, and expressed its intention to city planners. But the mayor and others were concerned about the city's deteriorating downtown area and knew that regardless of where the store located, it was of such outstanding caliber that it would not only attract customers to the new location, but other retailers would desire to be located near it. The city planners reasoned that if the retailer located the new store on the outskirts of town, the downtown area would lose its existing customer traffic and further precipitate its demise as other retailers relocated to capture the flow of traffic.

After several weeks of intense behind-the-scenes activity and an occasional news report or editorial on the matter, the retailer announced

(continued on next page)

that it would build its new store in the city center. Everyone involved seemed to express satisfaction and confidence in the city's booming downtown renewal project.

Later, after the new construction was underway, I had the opportunity to meet with the mayor. I congratulated him on such an outstanding achievement of getting the highly reputable retailer to lead the way to rejuvenating the downtown area. I then asked, "How were you able to swing this one?"

This man, who many regarded as having high ethical standards and person principles of conduct replied with evident embarrassment, "Do you know what it took to get that decision? It took $80,000 under the table."

When I asked him what he meant, he was unwilling to go into detail. He mentioned a few vaguely worded items such as waiving normal utilities fees, deferring taxes, and "other items."

Under the dictionary definition of bribery, were the city's actions in influencing the retailer's decision bribery? It certainly appears so, but no one dares call it bribery. After all, the term bribery seems so harsh for what we commonly accept as good, old-fashioned business savvy—the ability to get the job done, "whatever it takes."

expenses—they would be hard-pressed to justify such expenditures to stockholders.

If businesspeople feel that this definition of bribery is not appropriate, then we must search for a new definition that distinguishes between gifts and favors that are bribery and those that are not. Or, as we discussed with certain kinds of lies, we could identify gifts and favors that are "acceptable bribery" and "unacceptable bribery." Regardless of our approach, the status quo gives us nothing but a slippery slope to negotiate. At the top are acceptable acts of giving favors for acceptable levels or influence and somewhere near the bottom is blatant bribery —with no identifying marks, signs, nets, flags, or guardrails indicating where "acceptable bribery" ends and "unacceptable bribery" begins. This lack of definition, combined with the pressure for results and our own self-interests, tends to guide our business conduct right down the slope with no counterforces to alert our consciences that we are approaching—or have crossed—the line.

■ START HERE, NOW

This is such a challenging part of integrity that simple rules will not cut it. Nevertheless, if you're striving for a house of integrity, one has to start somewhere. Here are some suggestions. Keep in mind this is a process, not an event.

- **Acknowledge** to yourself and discuss with your management team the law of obligation and how it facilitates bribery.
- **Develop** a vocabulary for discussing the subject, including a definition of bribery. Start with the dictionary definition. If that doesn't work, develop a definition that works for your institution.

- **Differentiate** between acceptable obligations and unacceptable obligations for your organization.
- **Discuss** specific incidents with your team often and long enough that mutual understanding occurs and the appropriate values become ingrained.

CASE: THE PAYOFF[15]

A building contractor explained how he used the law of obligation to his advantage:

In the course of my work I regularly pay off town council members, though not in money. Contracting depends on time. If you need a subdivision approved or a section rezoned, you simply can't wait around until your case reaches the town meeting in the ordinary course of events. With a little help the case can be put on the next meeting's agenda and voted on quickly. This help consists in offering, say, a bricklaying job to one of the council members who is in the business. That person gets the case on the agenda and uses his or her influence to follow up and see that the decision is favorable. Then I send Christmas presents to the council member to let the person know that I remember the favor with gratitude. Council members are always looking for such jobs and gifts.

There really isn't anything dishonest in this practice. I never ask for anything unreasonable in the approval of subdivisions or the rezoning of sections, and I do not harm the town in that respect. And the council member's work in laying bricks, or whatever the job happens to be, must be up to par, or the person's business reputation will be ruined. I have never had to complain about the quality of work that I have given out to a council member, and I have never heard any complaints about the council's decisions in my favor, except from those who stood to gain by impeding civil progress. All I do is buy time, to everyone's benefit.

1. Is this a case of bribery? How is it or is it not?

2. Are the council members obligated to the contractor because of his favors? If so, in what way?

3. From the council members' point of view, do such favors constitute conflicts of interest?

4. What should the contractor do in these situations? What should the council members do? Why?

5. If you were a citizen in this community and knew about such practices, what would you do about it?

CHAPTER ELEVEN

Trust: When is a Promise a Promise?

"MY WORD IS MY BOND" is a phrase often used by persons attesting to their trustworthiness. Trust is a critical aspect of integrity. Surely one would not be regarded as a person of integrity who could not be trusted. Trustworthy is one "worthy of trust, reliable." Trust is a "firm belief in the reliability or truth of a person."[1]

Recently, the CEO of a major insurance company asked me to spend two hours talking with his managers about integrity, specifically, trust. When I discuss this aspect of integrity I always ask, "Trusted to do what?" Trusted to do the right thing? To look out for my interests? To not mislead?

To give this discussion a point of focus, we will explore the role of keeping promises as a big, big part of trust and hence, integrity.

Little wonder that there are so many complaints in business that people cannot be trusted. "He doesn't keep his commitments," "She won't honor our contract," "That company never lives up to its end of the deal, but it won't pay you unless you live up to your end." Much of business advertising affirms this problem: "We give honest value," "A name you can trust," "You can depend on us," "If you don't need new brakes, we'll tell you so," "With us, the price you see is the price you get."

All of these ads play on the widespread concern that you can't always trust what a company says. Good advertisers and salespeople identify common customer concerns, and then capitalize on them in advertising and sales pitches. If skepticism about trust was not such a pervasive concern for customers, advertisers would be foolish to use it as leverage.

What do people mean when they say, "my word is my bond," or, "she is someone who keeps her commitments"? Is it like what Oliver North said during his campaign for the U.S. Senate? He admitted to reporters, "I acknowledged in an informal, off-the-record meeting with a handful of members of one committee and some staff that I had not told them everything they wanted to know." He confessed to "misleading" Congress, but still insists he never lied.[1] In a later press conference, when asked what he would do about the lack of honesty in Washington, D.C., particularly in light of his behavior in the Iran-Contra hearings, he reportedly said, "I was not under oath. I would require that everyone who testifies before Congress do so under oath."

Is my word my bond only when I am under oath or contract? Is my "word" only valid if I raise my arm to the square as in a court of law and swear on the Bible, or if I "cross my heart"? What if I cross my fingers as I speak? If I sign a contract, is it only binding if a staff of lawyers can't figure a legal way out of it or around it? Or, have I given my word when I lead someone to believe I will do something? If we have verbal understanding, when does it become my "word"—after we nod our heads and say "yes" or "okay"? After we shake hands? After our attorneys draft a legal document and we both sign it? When the judge and jury say so?

There are two major elements to keeping promises that indicate a person's integrity: 1) The point at which a person acknowledges they have made a promise, and 2) when a person justifies breaking a promise.

■   **1. WHEN IS A PROMISE A PROMISE?**

According to the dictionary, a promise is "a declaration that one will give or do or not do a certain thing; an indication of something that may be expected to come or occur."[2]

WHAT IS YOUR WORD WORTH?

I once served on the membership committee of a service club. One day the name of a prominent businessman was proposed for membership. As was usual with other applicants, the name was circulated among members for their reaction. More than one member protested. When the members were invited to explain their concerns, one person detailed his experience as a supplier to the man's business. Among other grievances, he cited specific examples in which he had contracted with the man to deliver the services for a specified price. After providing the services, the businessman would respond, "That service wasn't that valuable to us after all, so here is what we will pay," and wrote a check for a smaller amount. Hardly a man of his word.

(continued on next page)

Early in 1993, most people believed that a very sought-after basketball player would return to his university for one more year before turning professional. No one expected the budding superstar to stay till graduation, but many believed he wasn't ready for "the big time." Also, it appeared that he had indicated that he would return. He had not signed a contract, but his discussion with the coach and others regarding his plans for when he returned were so explicit people concluded he had committed to coming back. The understanding was so clear and the coach was so confident of the player's commitment, that he had saved a scholarship for him, and done nothing to recruit a replacement during the just-completed college recruiting period.

Then in the spring, the player announced that he would go professional rather than return to the university. Discussion swirled widely. Many expressed disappointment but understood that if he waited one more year, with talk of a possible salary cap on professional basketball teams, he could lose out on several million dollars. Others argued that even though he may have originally indicated he would return, circumstances had changed; you have to allow new circumstances to enter into decisions, especially when the new circumstances amount to that much money.

Others declared that his decision was simply indicative of our greedy society. They felt that trust is

(continued from page 142)

When asked why the member continued to do business with the man, he replied, "Well, his company does a lot of business with us, and we just have to put up with it." Other members of the committee spoke up about how honest they considered the man to be, and placed his name on the ballot for membership. When the votes were tallied, he had received more negative votes than anyone else had in years, but not enough to defeat his membership, so he was admitted to the club.

Curiously, not only did this noted businessman fail to keep his agreed-upon word, but a club that prides itself in the integrity of its members seemed to turn its head the other way when confronted with a specific incident of questionable integrity (i.e., be trustworthy).

Nevertheless it was very interesting to hear the private comments of committee members and others who evidenced some introspection, like, "That's not that unusual. It's just the nature of the business when competition gets tough." Another said, "After this incident I'm going back and have a discussion with our managers," and another confessed, "Actually at times my company, under pressure to cut costs, has behaved similarly."

too easily given short shrift when a better deal comes along. One person remarked, "In a greedy world where politicians won't keep their promises, where corporations hire teams of lawyers to find loopholes in contracts when agreements no longer look favorable, what a lesson this young man could have conveyed to the youth and adults of the world if he had stood before the world press and said, "This may cost me a few million dollars, but my word and honor is worth more than that." Frequently circumstances do change; when it happens is it all right to go back on a promise?

Contrast this example with another professional young man, an accountant I will call Hank. His father was a prominent businessperson in the community. One day as I was walking I met up with Hank's father, with whom I am acquainted. After an initial greeting, he said, "Do you know what Hank did? He upset his wife and the rest of us last week. He phoned a bank to get information about refinancing the mortgage on his house, and he obtained information about interest rates, closing costs, and other things. When he finished his conversation with the banker, he said, 'I'll be there in the morning.'

"When I heard about it, I told him to go see a banker friend of mine. He did, and found out he could save $400 in closing costs. But he refused to do business with my friend and save the $400. He said to me, 'I told the other bank I would be there in the morning, and I must keep my word.' Hell, that was only a casual comment, not a promise."

Whenever I relate this incident to others, I get mixed reactions. Some say, "He'll never make a successful businessman. You have to take advantage of every financial opportunity," or "That's foolish—he never made a promise or signed an agreement." Others say, "That's great, but too ideal to really work in this competitive world." Only a few say things like, "That's just what we need in our world: people who are willing to pay the price to keep their word and be worthy of trust."

So when *is* a promise a promise? The answer depends on where you draw the line about promise making. If you believe giving your word only happens under oath or when you sign a contract with two witnesses, it leaves people open to change their minds—sometimes at your expense. On the other hand, if you believe that you give your word when you allow someone to believe you will do something, then you must keep that word—even if a better opportunity comes along.

The value of someone's word as a dependable promise rests upon a continuum, depending on the person's belief about the nature of verbal contracts:

My word is my bond:

[———]
Only under oath   When I allow someone to believe

In order to elevate the level of trust in our businesses, we should place ourselves toward the right side of this continuum. Problems arise in business when one side says, "They promised me," and the other side says, "We made no promises." Sometimes, in these cases, one side believes a promise was made, but the other side never intended to make a promise. Other times, clever businesspeople manipulate language and implications that entice people to believe one thing, and even close the sale, but later reveal that nothing was ever promised, or that technically, the implied things only apply to certain circumstances that don't exist for this customer.

SENSITIVITY ABOUT UNDERSTANDING

People who are serious about integrity don't just hang onto the technical meanings of individual words. Instead, they sense or try to find out what the other party is understanding or concluding from a given exchange because they understand how selective perception influences how "promises" come to be. After all, as discussed in Chapter One, selective perception determines how people interpret a message—meaning that sincere people can intend to make no promise while the recipient sincerely believes a promise has been made.

For example, if a manager talks to a discouraged employee, he or she may say something like, "I'd really like to see you get a large bonus at the end of the year if our sales increase, assuming we can keep our costs down—especially if we can get that new product finished and you continue to demonstrate how you have added value to the company." Assuming the employee has a great need for the increased income, selective perception may cause the person to conclude, "The boss promised me a significant bonus." All the ifs, assumptions, and uncertainties mentioned by the boss may be ignored or "blanked out" because they make the bonus uncertain.

Managers who are unskilled in ethical behavior will assume that the employee understood the message just as it was delivered—with many contingencies. Later, they must cope with the employee's accusations of broken promises. Managers who are skilled in ethical behavior can sense how others could interpret such messages. In this case, they would go to extra lengths to correct any misunderstandings and make sure the employee recognizes up-front that the bonus is not a promise, but a desired result.

AVOID GLIB PROMISES

People who have questionable integrity often are glib about making promises and making inferences. Without serious thought or commitment, they are quick to say, "Oh yes, we can do that," or "Yes, I'll do that." Later when they find it difficult to keep their commitments, they back out. Sometimes they make casual comments that imply a promise though they have no intent of fulfilling it.

On the other hand, people who have genuine integrity are reluctant to make promises or even imply them. They think through what it would take to fulfill a pledge before they make it—or at least consider whether it is within their power to keep the promise and whether they are willing to put forth the effort to complete the obligation. They consider it abhorrent for people to make casual or glib promises or commitments when there is no serious intent of following through. They consider their word a sacred treasure that they do not give out lightly or without thought. Such people of integrity, more often than not, carefully estimate their promises with regard to scheduling and financial forecasts, and then try to fulfill their promises early and under-budget if they can—giving apologies, occasional concessions, and plenty of advance notice if they find they can't. They often go to great lengths to keep their word, even when others consider the promises inconsequential.

■ 2. WHEN IS IT JUSTIFIED TO BREAK A PROMISE?

One of the most vexing challenges for buisinesspeople who want to keep their word is to determine what to do when circumstances change. Sometimes we make commitments to do certain things, but something unexpected comes up, making it difficult, if not impossible, to keep the original promises.

Suppose Robert says he will attend a meeting on Friday, but on Wednesday he is admitted to the hospital after a serious stroke. Most of us would acknowledge that this would justify his failure to keep the commitment. We would not criticize him at all for not appearing at the meeting. But suppose Rebecca, from Chicago, agrees to make a public presentation at 8:30 a.m. on the morning of the fourteenth of next month in Kansas City. She arrives at the airport on the evening of the thirteenth and finds that her flight has been canceled and no other flight is going to Kansas City that night nor early enough for the meeting the next morning. Is she excused from missing the meeting, and if so, would she still be considered a person of her word? Probably most would say yes. After all, she did the best she could, and she had no way of knowing the flight would be canceled, right?

But Rebecca herself would disagree. For her, a promise is a promise. She asks the travel agent to check the availability of all flights into Kansas City from other cities that she could connect with from Chicago tonight. Still no luck. Then she checks the prices of a private jet, but it's too expensive for her and the group to which she will be making the presentation. The bus and train are available, but she fears they would make too many stops and not arrive in time. Finally, she decides that if she leaves now, she could drive overnight and arrive in time to get two hours of sleep before the presentation. To keep her commitment, she drives the whole way and, on two hours of sleep, makes her presentation at considerable personal cost, effort, and sacrifice.

Was Rebecca's effort beyond the call of duty? Did she exert more than she needed to just to keep her promise? Couldn't she simply have called and canceled the presentation? Could someone who wanted to keep his or her word do less? What would Abraham Lincoln have done? If you were part of the group that was to hear Rebecca's presentation, how would you feel about dealing with her in the future? Is she silly, or is she just doing what she said she would do? Should Rebecca be held up as an example for MBA students? For employees in your institution?

By acknowledging that some circumstances would justify our failure to keep a promise, we maintain a certain level of sanity and comfort. We can even maintain that we are people of our word, and that our word is our bond. But how large a price must we pay or how much personal sacrifice must we endure to honestly claim that we did our very best to keep a commitment? What circumstances would allow you to justifiably change your mind, back out of an agreement, or go back on your word? When circumstances change, are you justified in changing your mind, or is that a violation of your promise? What if a million dollars or more were involved? What if it could be done legally? Should you keep your word or fulfill a contract only when it doesn't cost anything more than you first expected? Or should you keep your word at all costs?

A good measure of the value of a person's word is how much he or she is willing to give up to keep a promise or commitment. Would everyone be willing to break their word if they were given the right price? Just as beliefs about the nature of verbal contracts relate to the value of a person's word, beliefs about when it is acceptable to allow circumstances to change an agreement impact the strength, and also the value, of a person's word as a dependable promise.

If circumstances relating to my commitment change, I am willing to change my mind:

[————————————————————————————————————]

Whenever it's to my advantage   Only when it's impossible to keep
                                          my original agreement

Again, the farther right on the continuum we tend to place our marks, the more trust people can place in our words. However, moving closer to the right also implies having much greater amounts of information at hand when we make our commitments. How far people are willing to go and how much they are willing to sacrifice to carry out a promise are good indicators of how much they believe in the phrase, "My word is my bond."

WHAT PRICE HONOR?

Peter is a reputable drywall taper. In the construction of a home or a building, when the frame has been put up and the electricity, plumbing, and ventilation ducts have been installed, a drywall crew comes to attach sheets of drywall to the inside walls. Then a taper smoothes the walls by filling in cracks and holes and shaping corners with drywall tape and spackle. Peter is so good that when he is done most people cannot detect where the joints are. Over the years several contractors had employed Peter to finish off drywall jobs.

Peter loved to talk about a man named Larry who was the best drywall contractor he had ever worked for. Peter described Larry like this:

> Larry has never missed a payroll in twenty years. Even when he hasn't been paid on time, Larry will go to the bank and borrow money rather than be late with a paycheck. In this business, it's common to have your pay delayed because a contractor hasn't been paid yet or some other excuse. But not with Larry: With him you know your pay will be there when scheduled or before. Larry is a man of his word.

When I was in my teens, I had a job driving a truck. One evening, when a half-dozen of us truck drivers stopped to eat at a cafe, the group began to tell some trucking stories. One driver, Ed, told how he had purchased a large wrench from Sears-Roebuck. "They told me it was guaranteed," he said. "If anything goes wrong with it, just bring it back, and we'll replace it," they told me. He continued:

Well, one day I was trying to remove a flat tire from my rig, and one of the lug nuts was stuck. I put that big wrench on it, and it still wouldn't budge. Finally, I found about a four-foot piece of heavy pipe and attached it to the wrench handle to get some leverage. I laid it out just about horizontal. Then, with all my 215 pounds, I jumped on the end of the pipe and something gave way. I went over to the wheel to check the lug nut, but it was still in place—the wrench had broken. I should have known that much leverage could break anything.

A lumber company in Maine had promised a charitable organization that it would donate the materials, valued at about $33,000, for the organization to build a log cabin. The charity could then auction off the cabin to raise funds or use it for events, as it saw fit. But shortly after the company made the promise, the lumber company's plant burned to the ground. The financial losses were so great that the company would likely go under. The reporter, who was aware of the company's promise to the charity, prodded, "I guess this means the charity will lose a major donation. That's too bad."

"No," responded the company owner. "They will still get their building materials just as we promised."

But I remembered them saying I could bring the wrench back. I knew they wouldn't replace it because of the unreasonable abuse I had put it through, but I couldn't afford another wrench, so I thought it would be worth a try to see just how good their promise was. Well, I took that dang wrench in. They looked at it and said, "Well, that won't do you any good." They never asked me any questions, just handed me a new wrench. It's hard to believe they meant exactly what they said.

GETTING AROUND A PROMISE

A businessman I will call Bjorn Sedgewick, owned a successful silver mine. Another man, (I'll call him Ian Belz) made a mining claim on a piece of land adjacent to Sedgewick's. Apparently, Sedgewick's mine began to extend into land claimed by Belz, and Belz pointed it out. Sedgewick proposed, "I will put up the money for extending the mine into your property if you will operate the venture, and we will each hold a 50 percent interest in the mine." Belz agreed, and the venture got underway. Each subsequent day showed that the venture would be profitable for years to come.

After some time passed, Sedgewick came up with another idea. He told Belz,

"I've located a mining engineer who could really be helpful in our mining operation. I believe I can get him to join us for a portion of ownership in the mine. If you will give me 2 percent for your 50 percent, I would put it with 2 percent of my part and offer it to him. That would give him 4 percent ownership, and we would each retain 48 percent."

Belz agreed and signed over 2 percent of his ownership to Sedgewick for the offer. Time went by, and when no engineer appeared Belz confronted his partner about the arrangement. Sedgewick admitted that there never had been an engineer, but that he had used the ruse to gain control of the mine—he now owned 52 percent of the stock and controlling interest in the mine.

According to the attorney who represented Belz in a subsequent lawsuit, when Belz challenged Sedgewick in court, Sedgewick responded, "Unless you are willing to do that to your own mother, you won't succeed in business."

People who take this approach to the law and to their business partners are only focused on producing results. When it comes to keeping promises, gaming ethics often seem to be the favorite tool. For them, abandoning a promise or pulling out of a deal is appropriate not only when money is at stake but also whenever they can gain an advantage by doing so.

Was Sedgewick just being shrewd? In business circles, I have many times heard one executive refer to another as being shrewd in a tone of admiration. According to the dictionary, admiring a person who exhibits shrewdness merits approval. "Shrewd: having or showing sound judgment and common sense, clever."[3]

One day while talking with one of *Money Magazine*'s "400 Wealthiest," I asked him if I should teach my university students to always be honest.

His reply: "Yes," then after a pause, "but tell them to do it shrewdly." Is being shrewd compatible with having integrity? Surely you should discuss this matter with the members of your organization. People of integrity do.

WHEN IT HURTS A LOT

Those who want to be worthy of trust should think twice about how quickly they would forgo solemn vows. They should ask themselves, "How large a price am I willing to pay to earn someone's trust?" "How much am I willing to show that I can be trusted to keep my word?" The world of business is a good place to start.

For those who would aspire to an organization of integrity, take time to explore and discuss in detail these two major ingredients of trust: 1) When have I made a promise? and 2) When am I justified in breaking that promise? Don't just talk in vague generalities, but discuss specific incidents like the case at the end of this chapter, "A Better Offer."

In working with other people maybe it would help to not categorize them under one of two broad labels, "trustworthy" or "not trustworthy," but to look at ourselves and others on a scale of trust, as one who can be trusted:

- in most things
- or in many things
- or in some things
- or in few things
- or seldom.

CASE: A BETTER OFFER

During the month of February in the last term of his MBA program, Greg was interviewing with various companies and looking for a good opportunity to launch his career. He was offered a good position with a prominent company in Dallas that had an international reputation for producing high-quality products—probably the highest quality in the industry.

Greg and his wife traveled to Dallas at the company's expense to meet with company officers and take a look around. After he returned to school, Greg told the interviewer over the phone that he had decided to accept the company's offer and would move to Dallas as soon as he finished his degree at the end of June. At this point, he had not signed anything or written an acceptance letter. The company was delighted to have Greg on its team since he was a bright and highly motivated young man. They began to make preparations for his arrival.

A little over two weeks later, another company made an offer. Greg had visited the other company in Atlanta before his trip to Dallas, but he thought the company had lost interest. Although the money was about the same as the Dallas position, the Atlanta assignment would be better for Greg's career goals, offering him the kind of experience he would need to pursue his career path. After considerable deliberation and consultation with friends and a few of his favorite professors, Greg accepted the new offer, notifying the company in Atlanta of his decision in a letter. He then penned a note to the interviewer in Dallas to tell him that he had changed his mind and would not be accepting the position there.

QUESTIONS

1. Did Greg do the right thing?

2. When is a promise a promise? Did Greg make a promise?

3. Was Greg a man of his word in this incident?

4. How far should a person go, or how much should a person sacrifice just to keep a promise?

5. Was Greg justified in going back on his word to the company in Dallas?

6. In business, is it acceptable to follow whatever is the best course for you personally? If you don't look out for yourself, who else will?

ALLOW THAT LYING IS
SOMETIMES THE RIGHT
THING TO DO

CHAPTER TWELVE

Is Lying Sometimes the Right Thing to Do?

NOT LONG AGO, I attended a lunch for one of Rotary International's large clubs. While I was visiting with a senior executive of a large bank who was sitting at my right, the conversation turned to business ethics.

"Is lying sometimes the right thing for an honest person to do?" I asked him. Before he could answer, the CEO of a manufacturing company who was sitting on my left and who had not been involved in the conversation, blurted out, "Absolutely not!"

Turning in his direction I responded, "Why not?"

He said, "Lying is always wrong under any circumstance."

"Do you have any children?" I asked him.

"Yes, we have five."

"And what did you tell them at Christmastime about Santa Claus?"

"Well . . ." he said in a subdued tone.

I asked the two men a series of questions:

• Would you lie to save your country from a dictator?
• Would you lie to win a war?
• Would you lie to save a child's life?

- Would you lie to preclude your company from bankruptcy and preserve 1,500 jobs for the community?
- Would you lie to preclude serious embarrassment for you, your company, or your family?
- Would you lie to avoid hurting someone's feelings?
- Would you lie to help a child struggling with his or her self-image?

The questions were followed by a pause, and then the CEO observed, "I guess I need to rethink this whole matter."

When confronted with these questions, people are prone to say, "Well I might stretch the truth a little, but I wouldn't lie," or "I wouldn't say everything, but I wouldn't lie." Our society is so steeped in the "never tell a lie" platitude, that we go through wonderfully creative mental gymnastics to assure ourselves we are living the platitude. We forget that to tell the truth is not just to state the facts but to convey a true impression, and try to keep our conscience clear by labeling it anything but what it is—a lie. In the end, it is better that you acknowledge at least to yourself that sometimes lying is appropriate and have justifiable moral reasons for doing so, than to deceive yourself that there was no falsehood.

▪ EVERYONE JUSTIFIES LYING AT TIMES

The truth is, lying sometimes is a legitimate part of life and business. Acknowledging this, at least to oneself, is part of developing integrity. Discussing this aspect of integrity is in no way intended to encourage lying; on the contrary, it is intended to prevent glib deceptions by helping people make more conscious, moral decisions.

One of the traditional examples frequently cited is Nazi Germany. If you were secretly harboring a Jewish family in your home in Germany and the Nazis knocked on your door asking if there were any Jews in the house, would you lie? Most people quickly reply that lying would surely be the right thing to do.

Who of you sending a son or daughter off to a career of spying with the FBI or CIA would admonish him/her to always be honest and kind or polite with everyone they meet?

Obviously spying, war, and other human calamities are extraordinary circumstances, and exceptions to values respecting truth are justified. Challenges to pure integrity, however, come closer to ordinary lives and occur in the course of normal everyday living. The leaders of business, government, and other institutions are often faced with circumstances, like negotiations, where being open, honest, and forthright may just not be appropriate.

■ THE NOBLE LIE

One of the major traps that tends to draw aspiring honest people from the path of integrity is the noble lie, where the ends are so noble that ignoble means are justified. In a study about what personality traits makes for great U.S. presidents, a poll of 719 historians ranked the top nine presidents: 1) Abraham Lincoln, 2) Franklin D. Roosevelt, 3) George Washington, 4) Thomas Jefferson, 5) Theodore Roosevelt, 6) Woodrow Wilson, 7) Harry S. Truman, 8) Andrew Jackson and 9) Dwight D. Eisenhower. One of several results of the study states, "Great presidents are open to new ideas, and they question traditional values. They generally are not straightforward and stretch the truth when necessary."[1]

We learned during the Iran-Contra scandal of the 1980s about a concept known as "plausible deniability." Apparently, some of President Ronald Reagan's underlings felt it was important to keep certain truths from him so he could stand in public and honestly deny he'd had any knowledge of certain acts. These people reasoned it was so noble to preserve the president's image of integrity—so important to the country—that the deliberate deceit of the president was justified.

In politics we often see candidates deviously demonized by their opponents through vicious rumors, dirty campaign tricks, false accusations, and the twisting of statements. All this is justified by the opponents in the "noble" cause of saving our country or government from destruction at the hands of the other party or candidate. Similarly, in business, those in power frequently engage in cover-ups and make misleading statements because they feel that it's important to preserve the administration's positive image and keep "less qualified people" from taking over.

As one author wrote, "Those who say that lying has no place in business aren't telling the truth."[2] Even in the medical profession, "doctors need to lie sometimes," reported a study by the *Journal of the American Medical Association*:

> A team of physicians at Brown University in Providence, Rhode Island, surveyed 211 physicians to see whether they would lie in . . . hypothetical cases. . . .
>
> Physicians were asked if they would lie to an insurance company in order to help a patient obtain reimbursement for a routine mammogram, x-ray

used to detect early stages of breast cancer. [In the real world, a large number of health insurance plans do not cover the costs of preventative screening tests such as mammograms.]

In the hypothetical case, a healthy 52-year-old woman goes to her doctor for a routine physical exam. Her insurance plan will not pay for a mammogram, with one exception: If the doctor conducts the test because he thinks the patient might have breast cancer, the insurance company will cover the cost. Otherwise, the woman will have to pay $200 out of her own pocket.

[The question asked was:] Put yourself in the doctor's shoes. You have absolutely no reason to think your patient has cancer. Should you lie and write down on the insurance claim that the mammogram was performed to "rule out cancer?" Or should you tell the woman that if she wants the mammogram as part of her physical, she will have to pay for it herself?

Nearly 70 percent of the doctors surveyed said they would lie. . . . The duty to advocate in the interest of one's patient sometimes requires lying.[3]

A statement of Oliver Wendell Holmes, the famous doctor, jurist, and poet comes to mind, "We must teach our medical students to round the sharp corners of truth."

Or suppose a child is struggling with his self-image and has low self-confidence. He tries a significant new task, say a public performance, and does very poorly. Should you just be honestly frank? Or does the "noble" end of building self-confidence justify you in conveying an impression that the event wasn't as bad as it seemed to him? Should you select a minor good aspect of the experience and blow it up so that the child really feels that he did better than either of you actually think? What if you or someone else makes him feel good about the experience, and the boy decides to continue to try something that, had he been given your honest feedback, he gladly would have given up on? On the other hand, what if your blunt honesty causes the child to give up on something he wants with all his heart and could have developed as a talent had he continued?

When someone does a foolish thing that could be publicly embarrassing in a corporation—badly scarring the company's image or negatively affecting the stock price for thousands of stockholders—is a cover-up, or noble lie, justified? If the media begins to suspect something and point fingers, is deliberately denying the accusation, although it is true, justified? Should the company simply hire a good

A friend of mine, Cyril Figuerres, related to me a story of how his parents had withheld information about his ethnic background from him to protect his positive self-image.

When I was a young boy growing up in Lahaina, Maui, I loved reading comic books, especially about GI Joe. From comic books, I soon learned that the American soldiers were always the "good guys" who wore nicely fitted uniforms. They were courageous, fought cleanly, and were always victorious. In contrast, the Japanese soldiers were always the "bad guys" who wore baggy, dingy uniforms. They were cowards who fought with dirty tactics and always suffered defeat. Even the acoustical property of their respective rifles differed. The American rifles had a rapid, crisp sound: "rat-tat-tat-tat-tat." But, the Japanese rifles had a slow, sluggish sound: "buddha-buddha-buddha" (Perhaps the comic book writer thought the great Buddha was reincarnated as a Japanese rifle.)

My favorite pastime was to play GI Joe at the beach. My buddies and I would pretend we were attacking the beachhead, yelling, "Rat-tat-tat-tat-tat! Kill those dirty Japs!"

Then came the day of reckoning. One day, an older boy disrupted one of our exciting beach attacks and said to me, "Why you shooting the Japs? You neva know you one Jap?" (Translation: "You never knew you were Japanese?")

(continued on page 158)

public relations firm to put the best possible spin on the matter to minimize negative fallout? In such cases, how often do CEOs instruct their principal mouthpieces, "Now whatever you do, go out there and tell them the truth"? But are public relations firms hired to tell the truth?

So many times I have heard executives say "When everything is going well and there is plenty of cash in the bank, honesty is easy. When challenges arise, that is the test."

■ THE LITTLE WHITE LIE

Another major trap that haunts aspiring ethical people is the seductive "little white lie," or "it's just a fib." The thinking seems to be that whenever we tell a small,

(continued from page 157)

I protested, "No, I not one Jap!"

"Yes, you one Jap!" he insisted.

"No, I not!" I said. I absolutely refused to believe it.

The next day, I asked my schoolteacher, and she confirmed what the awful boy had claimed. I felt devastated. I didn't want to be a "dirty Jap."[4]

Cyril felt betrayed by his parents who had never told him about his heritage: His father was Filipino and his mother Japanese; he looked Asian. If you had been in his situation, would you have judged his parents as dishonest for withholding the truth about his ancestry? The way he tells the story, his parents had intentionally and willingly withheld the truth, which eventually resulted in devastating emotional consequences. Nevertheless, he knew their intent was pure and benevolent. They had spared him—and themselves—from dealing with one of the darkest periods of Japanese-American history during World War II, which involved America's betrayal of its Japanese-American citizens, the use of Japanese internment camps, and other atrocities. While in this case the cover-up seemed to backfire, Cyril grew up with a very good self-image—earning a Ph.D. from Purdue University, has been an excellent researcher, and has successfully carried out major leadership responsibilities in Japan and the U.S.A.

insignificant, no-one-gets-hurt kind of a lie, then lying could be the right thing to do. Teaching children about a Santa Claus who lives at the North Pole with elves and reindeer could be one example. Handing out unjustified compliments or flattery may be another example. But what about lying about your age by a year? What if a lie about age occurs on a driver's license application, and an underage driver hits the street in his father's souped-up Corvette?

President Dwight D. Eisenhower placed a great deal of emphasis on integrity in his career. He was a model of honesty, and that honesty was generally a key aspect of his public image. But Merle Miller, in his biography or him, gives clear evidence that Ike lied about his age on his application to West Point, though only by one year. Ike was aware that to get into the Naval Academy at Annapolis, he could not be older than nineteen, but he was twenty years old, and thinking that the same rule applied to West Point, he wrote on his application a date that showed him to be nineteen years old.[5]

Is this one of those deceptions that is so small and insignificant that it's okay? Besides, look at what his education and career enabled him to do in the service of his country and mankind. Does the promise of a good result or the hope of a better result justify the "little white lie?" In Eisenhower's case some may argue that he was justified. But had he not been so successful, would we still feel that it was okay for him to lie? As it turned out, the age requirements at West Point were different; an honest answer about his age would not have kept him out. But does this fact make the lie less significant and perhaps even more justifiable? When a person intentionally lies, is it not just as morally wrong whether it would make any difference in the outcome or not? Eisenhower's fudging by one year on his age is perhaps not significant. But with the limited admissions at West Point, if his lying had allowed Ike to occupy a slot that perhaps would have left some other honest young man out, how significant was the lie? What if that person had been able to accomplish an even greater work? We'll never know.

■ SO IS LYING SOMETIMES THE RIGHT THING?

According to one argument, even small lies are as morally corrupting as the big ones. The big ones may have far more devastating results, but the impact on society's moral fiber is no different.

So is lying sometimes the right thing for an honest person to do? The answer is yes. In fact, nearly everyone lies periodically with "good justification." Now that this fundamental question is out of the way and you can get on with reading this book, what skills are necessary to manage this phenomenon without becoming a pathological liar?

The guideline "I will never tell a lie," in light of what we have just discussed, is not possible. Just developing the skill of setting precise and useful guidelines is challenging. Here are two examples of such guidelines:

- "Lying is only justified under unusual and extraordinary circumstances." The few justifiable situations could be when human life is in jeopardy, and when a major institution, such as a church, university, or country is threatened. On the other hand, major embarrassments: loss of jobs, reputations, or contracts; sharp declines in stock value; and hurting people's feelings would generally not justify lying.

- "In many circumstances lying may be appropriate." These situations could be if the truth would hurt someone's feelings, cause the person to lose his or her job, cause great embarrassment to himself or herself or to the company, create a major loss of stockholders' money, disrupt the person's work group, or be seen as an act of disloyalty. In other words, whenever telling the truth would entail an economic or emotional cost, then lying is justified for that person, particularly when it is evident that the person will not get caught.

As there are no simple, pat answers to when lying is justified, maybe the following concept will help with the wrestle. Consider three general relationships between ends (your goal) and means (how you reach it):

NOBLE ENDS — IGNOBLE MEANS

ENDS: NOBLE

MEANS: BORDERLINE

1. The ends are noble and great compared to the means, which are questionable or borderline ethical.

ENDS: MODERATELY GOOD

MEANS: MODERATELY UNETHICAL

2. The ends and the means are balanced in their degree of value and ethicalness.

ENDS: OF QUESTIONABLE VALUE

MEANS: IGNOBLE

3. The ends are only of minor value compared to the means which are grossly unethical.

Under these three scenarios, we can begin to set some reasonable guidelines about when questionable means may be justifiably employed to obtain some end:

1) The ends may justify the means only when the ends are many times greater in value than questionable means.
2) Whenever the ends and means are roughly the same weight of value, the means are rarely justified, if ever.

3) When the ends have little value compared to the gross wrong of the means, the means should never be justified.

So it is not the absolute value of good or bad that matters, but the relative balance or imbalance between the two. That is, an end may have only moderate value, but if the means are only slightly over the line they may be justified in some cases.

◼ MOVE TOWARD INTEGRITY

Businesspeople must really wrestle with this concept and figure out for themselves and for their companies when lying is justified. Ignoring the issue will give rise to concerns about your personal integrity and that of your institution. Consider three suggestions:

- **1. Recognize and acknowledge that we all justify lying and deception under certain conditions.** This point is an essential key to doing something about ethical behavior. As long as a manufacturing CEO believes that people should always tell the truth but remains unaware that even he doesn't follow that guideline, he can do nothing to correct the situation. He will neither set conscious guidelines for himself that will give him direction as to when lying might be appropriate, nor will he police his own deceptions. We cannot correct unethical behavior if we are not even aware that we are engaging in it.

- **2. Understand the implications of assuming that lying is sometimes justifiable and appropriate.** Once we acknowledge that under some circumstances lying is acceptable, even if those circumstances are extremely rare, then arguing whether a person is honest or dishonest is a moot question, and further discussion of the issue is only wasted effort. If we admit that lying is sometimes okay, then claiming that we are honest people is a self-deception.

   To have an effective relationship with another person, having an understanding of the special circumstances in which that person or institution may be dishonest and when they will not, will do much to maintain a healthy working relationship. Predictability is one aspect of integrity.

- **3. Establish deliberate and conscious guidelines for when lying is justified in business and when it isn't.** If such lines are not clearly and consciously drawn, pressures rather than principles will dictate moral conduct. If there are no recognized guidelines, then no one can ever tell when a person is being honest or not. Stop mouthing the "always be honest" slogan and start talking about when it is okay to lie. Talk, talk, talk! Discuss the questions at the beginning of this chapter. Discuss specific incidents from your organization's experiences. Talk specific issues until everyone has an ingrained sense of what is justified and what is not in your institution.

CASE: MOVING TO MEXICO

The Barton Textile Factory was a major employer in a small midwestern town. There were three hundred people on the payroll, and although the jobs were not really high-paying, the typical $6 per hour wage helped many families make ends meet in this rural part of the state.

Competition in the clothing industry was very intense, and margins were very tight, but the operation had always been profitable. But the owners learned that they could open a factory in Mexico where they could hire as many employees as they needed for only $.60 per hour, a move that would significantly increase profits for the company, and eliminate the advantage other manufacturers had who were already manufacturing offshore.

To keep from killing the morale of the employees, the announcement to

the public was kept secret until just two months before the owners decided to shut down the factory. Two months later, the factory closed on schedule, and the operation moved to Mexico. The town was devastated, as no other local employers could take up the slack.

QUESTIONS

1. Did the noble end—significantly enhanced profits—justify the ignoble means—leaving a town economically high and dry? Why?

2. Were the owners ethically responsible? In what ways were they? In what ways were they not?

3. Did the company owe the town anything? If so, what?

4. Should the owners have given the town a longer lead time, or at least let the employees know they were thinking about it? How early? Should they have given the town another month? More time than that?

5. Was management ethical to keep the move secret at all? Was it ethical to move the factory?

CHAPTER THIRTEEN

12 Principles in Review

"Some persons are likeable in spite of their unswerving integrity."

Don Marquis

IF YOU NOW FEEL that being a person of integrity is much more complicated than you have ever thought, or if you now feel less honest than you thought you were before, then the message of this book has started to get through. A lack of awareness is one of the conditions that allows honesty, trustworthiness, and other elements of integrity to suffer even among the most respected in our society. Improving societal integrity *does* begin with me even if it is only one or two more honest incidents a week.

It is easy to look at the big, public liars who have been indicted and think, "I'm sure I am not bad like they are. They are the ones causing morality's downward slide. Not me." That self-description is a major contributor to what many people see as a condition of weakening morality.

How often we take to ourselves a false sense of moral security by contrasting what we perceive as our own "small misdeeds" with the glaring violations of others that are revealed in the public press.

Looking to yourself as a place to start strengthening your business's morals and integrity is the beginning of improvement. Ignoring or denying your own responsibility to improve the business community's level of honesty will only reinforce the status quo. You may not be able to correct every wrong, but you can take the lead in setting a higher standard, if only in small ways. These small efforts can accumulate into a trickle of improved integrity. Several trickles will combine to form a stream. Many streams will merge to make a river of enhanced moral behavior in business.

Many people lament that integrity in our society is "going to hell in a hand-basket," that things are just getting worse and worse. Frankly, I doubt that is the case. The passage of time often dulls the vividness of sins past. If you refocus on the behavior of business executives and politicians of one hundred years ago, you'll find it a little hard to be convincing that actions today are worse than theirs were then. Modern communication has created a much greater general awareness of wrongdoing through the exposure in the printed and electronic media, and though the bright light of the public eye can make things seem worse, it also discourages would-be scammers with the fear of being found out.

But even if conditions are no worse than they were one hundred years ago, there is still an urgent need for significant improvement if our society is to sustain itself in an orderly, secure manner. Let's review the twelve keys that will help you.

- **KEY #1: RISE ABOVE TRITE SLOGANS THAT FEED SELF-DECEPTION.**

  Reciting slogans, labels, and platitudes such as "always be honest," or "I'm an honest person," not only fails to solve the problem, but also reinforces self-deception, which doesn't allow you or your company to see the truth. Meaningful discussion must replace slogan recitation.

- **KEY #2: AGREE ON A WORKING DEFINITION OF TRUTH TELLING.**

  Without a working definition, discussions of honesty most often are just talk. Robert Louis Stevenson's "To tell the truth is not just to state the facts, but to convey a true impression" is a good place to start. Even if you find it impossible to live up to it at all times, it is a good marker and a basis for meaningful dialogue.

- **KEY #3: BE WARY OF FOUR DEVICES OF DECEPTION.**

  Become aware of the variety of ways we all lie and deceive:
  1) By saying things that are not so. Most people agree this is lying. Many believe this is the only time they lie.

2) By overstating. Exaggeration or overstatement is deceitful because it does not convey a true impression.

3) By understating. This also conveys a false impression, but deserves separate mention because most of us attempt to minimize our role of responsibility when something goes wrong.

4) By withholding information. This may be the most common device of deception, and is the main device of the cover-up.

- **KEY #4: RECOGNIZE PRESSURE AS A MAJOR DETERMINANT OF HONESTY.**

The pressure to achieve desired results must be managed. Actions are not taken in a vacuum. In the competitive world there is a constant pressure, fueled by self-interest, to step over the ethical line and even the legal line.

- **KEY #5: BE ALERT TO INCREMENTAL MORALITY.**

Seldom does a person jump from being a choir boy to a criminal in a single leap. Most of it is a series of small, almost innocent steps that leads down to gross, dishonest behavior. With competitive pressure at our backs, once started down that slippery slope, it is difficult to draw the line and say "No, not one more 'innocent' step."

- **KEY #6: REALIZE THAT EVERYONE LIVES BY TWO DIFFERENT ETHICAL STANDARDS.**

In some parts of every person's life he or she lives by *personal* ethics. In other parts of every person's life he or she lives by *gaming* ethics. Clarify in life where one is appropriate and where the other is appropriate.

- **KEY #7: DEVELOP THE ESSENTIAL SKILLS FOR PERSONAL INTEGRITY.**

Desire alone does not an honest person make. Honesty requires at least two general skills: a) the ability to determine the truth and b) the ability to convey the truth accurately. Just as with any other skill, these skills require a major effort of practice, practice, practice.

- **KEY #8: RESOLVE CONFLICTS OF PRINCIPLE: THERE ARE NO GRAY AREAS.**

"That's a gray area" is a harmful label for a person of integrity to use. It keeps a person from seriously resolving the dilemma. Most gray areas are actually two right principles in direct conflict with each other. Establish a priority of principles for your organization. Deliberately choose the higher principle to obey. When loyalty and honesty are in conflict, loyalty will nearly always pay the greater dividend.

- **KEY #9: CREATE A CLIMATE WHERE WRONGFUL ACTS CAN BE REPORTED.**

There is a great need for more people to expose wrongdoing in organizations. However, from our youth we have been ingrained with, "Don't be a tattle tale." This cultural imperative causes well-intentioned whistle-blowers to be labeled disloyal, squealers, and worse. Set clear expectations for what to report, and how; reward the behavior you want.

- **KEY #10: UNDERSTAND THE LAW OF OBLIGATION.**

The law of obligation says you can accept no favor from another without incurring an obligation. Bribery can occur in many subtle ways because obligations arise often from supposedly innocuous practices such as letting someone pay for your lunch. A person of integrity does not acknowledge that someone did them a significant favor and then claim, "but it had absolutely no influence on my actions."

- **KEY #11: KNOW WHEN A PROMISE IS A PROMISE.**

First, learn to fully understand when a promise has been made. Is it only when a legal document has been drawn or is it when you allow someone to believe you will do something? Second, decide for you and your team what justifies failing to keep a promise and still preserve one's integrity when circumstances change.

- **KEY #12: ALLOW THAT LYING IS SOMETIMES THE RIGHT THING TO DO.**

Sometimes a lie is justified. Decide under what circumstances you would consider lying appropriate. Discuss them with your team, then stick to your standard.

Integrity is often thought to be a natural behavior and dishonesty an abnormal one. Actually, integrity is an attribute that must be learned and then meticulously cultivated until it has grown to its full capacity. After that a constant vigilance is required to sustain it. The bumps, rips, tears, and snares of everyday life will cause it to weather, decay, and disintegrate if constant maintenance, upkeep, and protection is not in place.

Integrity is not like gold that when found and locked safely in a treasure chest will last forever. It is more like a delicate gardenia, that unless continually protected, watered, weeded, and fertilized, its beautiful leaves will turn brown, die, fall off, and cease to fill the eye with beauty and the nostril with fragrance.

My hope is not that you will always be perfectly honest or an ideal model of integrity, but that you will, for two or three times each week, act with more integrity than you would have done had you not read this book.

NOTES

INTRODUCTION

1. Carolyn Kleiner and Mary Lord, "The Cheating Game," *U.S. News and World Report,* (November 22, 1999), p. 56.

2. Lorenzo Gracian [Baltasar Gracian y Morales], *Oráculo manual y arte de prudencia* [The Oracle Manual and Art of Prudence], Emilio Blanco, ed. (Madrid: Cátedra, 1995 [1647]); see also the English translation: *The Art of Worldly Wisdom,* Joseph Jacob, trans. (New York: Macmillan, 1956), cited in ibid, 47.

3. John Donne, "Devotions Upon Emergent Occasions," (8/12), (XVI Meditations 237).

CHAPTER ONE

1. John Abbot Worthley, "Compliance in the Organizational Ethics Context," *Frontiers of Health Service Management* 16, Winter (1999): 41.

2. Quinn McKay, "Red Flags Missed, Wrong Man Hired," *Business Horizons,* Summer 1963, 47–52.

3. Paraphrase from a 1995 speech by David J. Cherrington at Brigham Young University, Provo, Utah, used with permission. See Jeep Owen and David J. Cherrington, *Moral Leadership and Ethical Decision Making,* (Orem, UT: Legacy Foundation, 1997).

4. John A Byrne, "Phillip Morris: Inside America's Most Reviled Company," *Business Week,* November 29, 1999, 177.

5. Herbert Johnson, *Business Ethics,* 2nd ed. rev. (New York: Pitman Publishing Corp., 1961), 73.

CHAPTER TWO

1. Jerry Urseem, "Should You Lie," *Fortune Small Business,* (November 1999), p. 41.

2. Robert Louis Stevenson, "Truth of Intercoarse, in *Virginibus Pecerique and Other Papers* (New York: Charles Scribner's Sons, 1924), 56.

CHAPTER THREE

1. "Why doctors recommend Tylenol more than all leading brands combined," *Time,* 16 May 1977, 62.

2. "Makers of Tylenol, shame on you!" *Time,* 27 June 1988, inside front cover. Tylenol's ad is included within the same advertisement.

3. *The Tormont Webster's Illustrated Encyclopedia Dictionary,* (Montreal, QC: Toronto Publications, 1990), s.v. "Deception."

4. "Makers of Tylenol, shame on you!" *Time,* 27 June 1988, inside front cover.

5. Jerry Useem, "Should You Lie," *Fortune Small Business,* November 1999, 48.

6. Tom L. Beauchamp, "Manipulative Advertising," *Business and Professional Ethics Journal* Spring-Summer (1984): 12.

7. Jane Bryant Quinn, "New Handcuffs on the Cops," *Newsweek* September 3, 1984, 62.

8. Dean Foust and Spencer E. Ante, "When the CEO Is Too Good to Be True," *Business Week,* 16 July 2001, 62.

9. Bruce B. Auster and Josh Chetroynd, "Accentuating the Negative—Quietly. The new political ads: subtle, but stiletto sharp," *U.S. News and World Report* September 30, 1996, 43–44.

10. Herbert Johnston, *Business Ethics,* 2nd rev. (New York: Pitman Publishing Corp. 1961), 154.

11. Michael Deaver, as cited in Edward T. Pound, "White House Aide's Family Finances Brighten After Political Associates Help Wife Start Career." *Wall Street Journal* (Jan 3, 1985): A-36.

12. Tom L. Beauchamp's "Manipulative Advertising," 12.

13. Lee Berton, "Many Firms Hide Debt to Give Them an Aura of Financial Strength: Accounting Tactics Confuse Bank Lenders and Investors," *Wall Street Journal* (Dec. 13, 1983): A-1.

14. Herbert Johnston, *Business Ethics,* 2nd ed. rev. (New York: Pitman Publishing Corp., 1961), 113–14.

CHAPTER FOUR

1. Marsha (disguised name) in a student term assignment at the University of Utah, Dec. 2002.

2. Warren H. Schmitt and Barry Z. Posner, *Managerial Values in Perspective: An AMA Survey Report* (New York: American Management Association, 1983), 34–35.

3. Patricia Kitchen from *Newsday, Survey: Many Workers Unethical,* as published in *Salt*

Lake Tribune (8 April 1997): B-10. The study was conducted by the Ethics Officer's Association and the American Society of Chartered Life Underwriters and Chartered Financial Consultants.

4. Barbara Wood, cited in Associated Press article, "Win at All Costs Mentality Plaguing Livestock Shows," in *Deseret News* (Salt Lake City, March 20, 1994): A-11.

5. Karen Thomas, "Cheating, American Anthem: Land of the Fleece, Home of the Knave," a *USA Today* article in *Salt Lake Tribune* (2 Aug. 1995): A-1.

6. Chuck Gates, "SL Didn't Have a Moose's Chance For Games," *Deseret News* June 18, 1985

7. *Salt Lake Tribune,* June 13, 1999.

8. Nanette Byrnes, Richard A. Melcher and Debra Sparks, "Earnings Hocus-Pocus: How Companies Come Up With the Numbers They Want," *Business Week* October 5, 1998,134.

9. Herbert Johnston, *Business Ethics,* 2nd ed.rev. (New York: Pitman Publishing Corp., 1961) 94–95.

CHAPTER FIVE

1. John Curran, The Associated Press, "Not So Sweet, Ice Cream Cartons Hold a Little Less," *Salt Lake Tribune,* November 19, 2002.

2. Dean Faust, "Missing the Red Flags," *Business Week,* April 14, 2003, 72.

CHAPTER SIX

1. Benjamin Selekman, *A Moral Philosohy for Management,* (New York: McGraw-Hill, 1959), 101–2.

2. Edward P. Learned, "Multi-Products, Inc." Case Study number 307–114 (Boston, MA: Harvard Business School, 1959).

3. Albert Z. Carr, "Is Business Bluffing Ethical?:" *Harvard Business Review* January/February (1968): 143–53.

4. Linda Ashton, "Top Three U.S. Grocery Chains Sued Over Coloring in Salmon," *The Associated Press,* (reported in *Salt Lake Tribune,* Thurs. 24 April 2003): E-8.

5. Erin McClain, "Ex World Com CFO's Defense Is, "Everyone Was Doing It," *The Associated Press,* (*Salt Lake Tribune,* Wed. 23 April 2002): E-6.

6. Ibid.

7. Bob Mims, "As Justice—Lawyers Find TV Spots Good to Reach Clients," *Salt Lake Tribune,* February 17, 2003.

8. Machael Josephson, ed., "Ethical Obligations and Opportunities in Business: Ethical Decision Making in the Trenches." Monograph (Marina Del Rey, CA: The Joseph and Edna Josephson Institute for the Advancement of Ethics, 1988): 13.

9. Milton Friedman, "The Social Responsibility of Business Is to Increase Its Profits," *New York Times Magazine,* September 13, 1970, 32–33, 122, 124, 126.

10. *The Torment Webster's Illustrated Encyclopedia Dictionary,* (Montreal, QC: Tormont Publications, 1990), 66.

CHAPTER SEVEN

1. S. Leonard Rubenstein, "Points to Ponder," *Reader's Digest,* April 1985.

2. Carolyn Kleiner and Mary Lord, "The Cheating Game," *U.S. News & World Report,* November 22, 1999, 55.

3· *Oxford American Dictionary,* s.v. "Inquiry." Heald Colleges Edition Copyright 1980, Oxford University Press, Inc.

CHAPTER EIGHT

1. Eleanor Johnson Tracy, Peter van der Wicken, Susse G. Nayem, Sydney L. Stern, "In Love with Sweet Sixteen," *Fortune,* February 1975, 21.

2. Benjamin Selekman, *A Moral Philosophy for Management* (New York: McGraw-Hill, 1959), 101–2.

3. David Halberstam, "Their Call to Duty," *Parade Magazine,* July 7, 1985, 4–7.

4. Ralph Nadar, Peter J. Pethas, and Kate Blackwell, eds. *Whistle-Blowing: The Report of the Conference on Professional Responsibility* (New York: Grossman Publishers, 1972).

5. Richard Jaroslovsky and Paul Bluestein, "Feldstein is Put Under Intense Pressure for Publicly Voicing Qualms on Economy," *Wall Street Journal* December 1, 1983.

CHAPTER NINE

1. (The anguish David Kaczynski felt about reporting his brother was detailed in an Associated Press article, "Dilemma, Duty to Country or Family Loyalty?" in *Salt Lake Tribune* (5 April 1996) A-17).

2. Roger Nazeley, Letters to the Editor, *CFO: The Magazine of Senior Financial Executives,* November 1992, 9. Roger Nazely is from Philadelphia, Pennsylvania.

3. [Name Withheld], Letters to the Editor, *CFO: The Magazine of Senior Financial Executives,* November 1992, 5 and 7. The author is from Jessup, Georgia.

4. [Name withheld] Letters to the Editor, *CFO: The Magazine of Senior Financial Executives,* November 1992, 7. The author was unwilling to identify even where he/she was from.

CHAPTER TEN

1. *The Tormont Webster's Illustrated Encyclopedia Dictionary.* (Montreal, QC: Tormont Publications, 1990), s.v. "Obligation."

2. *The Tormont Webster's Illustrated Encyclopedia Dictionary.* (Montreal, QC: Tormont Publications, 1990), s.v. "Duty."

3. The death of Joseph Mengele, "The Angel of Death" was confirmed by genetic testing in 1992. See an Associated Press article, "Genetic Testing Confirms That Mengele Died in 1979," in *Deseret News* (April 8, 1992): A-1

4. Margaret Loeb, "Church Stirs Debate Over Tobacco," *Wall Street Journal,* May 8, 1984.

5. Mario Puzo, *The Godfather* (New York: Signet, 1978).

6. Eugene M. Bricker, "Sounding Board: Industrial Marketing and Medical Ethics," *New England Journal or Medicine* June 22, 1989, 1691.

7. Doug Podoswky and Richard J. Newman, "Prescription Prizes," *U.S. News & World Report*, March 29, 1993, insert on page 58–59.

8. David Rogers, "Senator [David] Durenberger Got Huge Campaign Gifts From Firms He Aided," *Wall Street Journal* April 24, 1984.

9. Lord David Ivor Young, as cited in George Gedda, "Anti-Bribery Worldwide Effort to Clean up Greased Palms" *Salt Lake Tribune,* February 13, 1996.

10. Peter Schnuck, "The Curious Case of the Indicted Meat Inspectors," *Harper's Magazine,* September 1972, 81.

11. Joseph B. White, "Comfy Ride: Car Magazine Writers Sometimes Moonlight for Firms They Review," *Wall Street Journal,* May 15, 1990.

12. Ellen E. Schultz, "More Crooked Planners Play on Fear, Scare up Cash," *Wall Street Journal,* April 26, 1991.

13. Todd Mason, "When Buying a Home Beware of Hidden Incentives to Brokers," *Wall Street Journal,* April 29, 1991.

14. *The Tormont Webster's Illustrated Encyclopedia Dictionary.* (Montreal, QC: Tormont Publications, 1990), s.v. "Bribery."

15. Herbert Johnson, *Business Ethics,* 2nd ed. rev. (New York: Putnam Publishing Corp, 1961), 282.

CHAPTER ELEVEN

1. *Oxford American Dictionary,* s.v. "Trustworthy," "Trust."

2. See an Associated Press article, *"North Says He Misled Probers But Didn't Lie."* In *Deseret News* (Oct. 6, 1994): A-19.

3. *Oxford American Dictionary* Heald College Edition Copyright 1980, Oxford University Press , s.v. "Shrewd," p. 716.

CHAPTER TWELVE

1. *What Makes a Great President?* as reported in the *Salt Lake Tribune,* Monday, 17 Feb 2003, p. A6.

2. Jerry Useem, "Should You Lie?" *Fortune Small Business,* November 1999, 43.

3. Arthur Kaplan, "Doctors Need to Lie Sometimes" *Salt Lake Tribune* (June 11, 1989).

4. Excerpt from a 1980 speech written and presented by Cyril Figuerres. Notes in the author's possession, used with permission.

5. Merle Miller, *Ike the Soldier: As They Knew Him* (New York: G.P. Putnam's Sons, 1987), 114.

BOTTOM